Sister
to Sister

Volume 2

Sister to Sister

Volume 2

Devotions

for and from
African American Women

Edited by Linda H. Hollies

Judson Press
Valley Forge

Sister to Sister, Volume 2:
Devotions for and from African American Women
© 1999 by Judson Press, Valley Forge, PA 19482-0851

Bible quotations in this volume are: TLB from *The Living Bible,* copyright © 1971. Used by permission of Tyndale House Publishers, Inc., Wheaton IL 60189. All rights reserved. NASB from the New American Standard Bible, © 1960, 1962, 1963, 1968, 1971, 1972, 1973, 1975, 1977 by The Lockman Foundation. Used by permission. KJV from *The Holy Bible,* King James Version. NIV from HOLY BIBLE: *New International Version,* copyright © 1973, 1978, 1984. Used by permission of Zondervan Bible Publishers. NKJV from The New King James Version. Copyright © 1972, 1984 by Thomas Nelson Inc.

NRSV from the New Revised Standard Version of the Bible, copyright © 1989 by the Division of Christian Education of the National Council of the Churches of Christ in the United States of America. Used by permission. All rights reserved. RSV from the Revised Standard Version of the Bible, copyright © 1946, 1952, 1971, by the Division of Christian Education of the National Council of the Churches of Christ in the U.S.A. Used by permission. THE MESSAGE. Copyright © 1993, 1994, 1995. Used by permission of NavPress Publishing Group. CEV from the Contemporary English Version. Copyright © 1991, 1992, 1995 by American Bible Society. Used by permission.

Library of Congress Cataloging-in-Publication Data
(Revised for volume 2)

    Sister to sister : devotions for and from African American Women
    Volume 2 editor is Linda H. Hollies
    Volume 1 editor was Suzan D. Johnson Cook

        p.   cm.
      1. Afro-American women—Prayer-books and devotions—
English.
    BV4844.S545 1995
    242'.643'08996073—dc20   95-19350
        ISBN 0-8170-1221-4 (pbk. : volume 1)
        ISBN 0-8170-1318-0 (pbk. : volume 2)

Printed in the U.S.A.
06 05 04 03 02 01 00 99
10   9   8   7   6   5   4   3   2   1

Dedication

How rich and glorious is the portion God offers us. . . . How vast are the resources of God's power open to us who have faith.
—Ephesians 1:18–19

This work is dedicated to the rich, glorious, and vast network of healing links who have empowered my life with their unconditional love, tender care, and constant prayers.

My parents, James and Doretha Adams;
Big Mama, Eunice Wade and Uncle Dock, and Surrogate Dad Uncle Clint and Aunt Barbara;

Barbara Jean Vinson, Elizabeth Clark, Darlene Sims, grade school sisterhood;

Thelma Pryor, Madine Blakely Randolph, Yvonne Frank, church sistahood;

Hortense House and Della Burt, teacher-professor-mothers-friends;

Emma Justes, Emilie Townes, Helen Fannings Ammons, seminary hook-up;

Eleanor Miller, Daisybelle Thomas Quinney, Terrill Cistrunk, Janet Hopkins, Harlene Harden, Vera Jo Edington, Ida Easley, Frankella Brandon, Andris Salter, Joyce E. Wallace, Alberta Petrosko, Beverly Garvin, and *all* the sisters who are Woman to Woman Ministries, Inc.;

and Lucille Brown, Ruby Earven, and Ray Margaret Jackson, my motherhood circle!

Contents

Ricne Adams-Morris

Foreword

I loves me some Sister Chris!
She's energetic, graceful, kind, inspirational,
  and just fun to be around.
A natural born encourager, she lights up the
  church
just by that beam on her face which is her ever
  ready smile.
Sister Chris has a wonderful, loving husband,
  seven adoring children, and loads of grandchildren who depend on her as much as her
  church family does. . . .
The doctors say there is nothing they can do for
  the cancer in her spine.

I loves me some Mama Geneva!
When my mom died, Mother Geneva Riddle
  was right there to comfort,
to care, to scold, and to console.

We go on trips, share hotel rooms at conferences,
    go shopping,
and do other things that Mom and I didn't have
    time or money to do.
The doctors seem to be losing the battle with
    the cancer that has attacked her throat.

I loves me some Uncle Clint!
My mother's second brother is the one I called
    "Uncle Bitey Boy."
When I was growing up he would pay me a dol-
    lar to bite my chubby cheeks.
And, he never bit hard either!
He was the uncle who would join me on the
    floor for a game of jacks
or would rig up the jump rope and turn it for
    me when no one else wanted to play.
As time has passed, Uncle Clint is still the one
    to join in the fun
or provide solutions and common sense to my
    problems.
The doctors say that pancreatic cancer is always
    terminal.

My friend of twenty years says that he has lung
    cancer.

How can I begin a time of devotion with all these
   situations
that bring mental anguish, pain, and confusion?
These are things over which I have no control!
As I cry out in prayers for healing of my loved
   ones,
I discover that my first need is to be comforted
   myself.
Before we can begin to be of comfort to others,
   we need to find someone.
But who can understand our selfish side without condemnation?

Comfort comes when the Sisters gather.

**Essential Thought: Even when your
gray skies turn black, the Son still
shines!**

   Riene Adams-Morris is a poet, evangelist, and member of Liberty Temple Church of God in Christ in Gary,
Indiana. She teaches in the Gary Public School system
and is a program counselor specializing in forward
movement of the mentally and physically challenged.
She is mother of two sons and a grandmother.

Acknowledgments

Without the brothers, there would be no sisters!

Rev. James Anderson, my father in ministry;

Rev. Willie Clay and Dr. Robert Johnson, my ministry promoters;

Rev. William "Bill" Cull and Rev. David Brewster Nelson, my ministry instructors and mentors;

Bishop Jonathan D. Keaton, my brother, intercessor-questioner-friend;

Bishop Donald Ott, my denominational guide and encourager;

Dr. Zawdie K. Abiade, Rev. Anthony Earl, Dr. Michael Carson, Dr. Dennis Robinson, Rev. Donald Guest, brothers, friends, and back-ups;

Mista Chuck! Charles H. Hollies, my mighty, mighty good man!

And,

Mr. Eric Thorsen, my handy dandy, smiling, trusty, swirling, twirling, efficient, loving, hardworking, detailed, caring, and competent administrative assistant!

Introduction

A Gathering of the Sisters

I moved again! Studies have determined that having to move is one of the great traumas of our lives. It really is a stress filled occasion to pull up stakes, pack up your life's belongings, and live in transition. My family is familiar with my itinerant life style. Therefore, we have developed a system. We have an established method. We have a well-arranged routine. After the movers get me into the new house, my sisters come.

My sisters are familiar with my house. My sisters are acquainted with my possessions. My sisters know the contents of my cabinets and closets. During the last move, one of my girlfriends came over to offer help when the movers left. I was so tired that I couldn't even provide her with instructions. So, I simply thanked her for showing up and informed her, "My sisters are coming tomorrow." I knew that when they arrived, things would be in order. I knew that the chaos of boxes would disappear. And, I knew that beauty would be established as this new house took on my character and became "home." Order was my manifest destiny because my sisters were coming!

Jacquie, Riene, and Baby Sister, Jeannie, arrived early the next morning, ready for work. I was prepared for their arrival. Food was on the stove, and the boxes had been well marked with labels. The large pieces of furniture were in place. My sisters toured the space. Afterwards, we sat at the kitchen table, ate the meal I had prepared, and shared my vision of what I hoped to achieve. Then we got up and went to work. My sisters came. When they left, a house had been made a home.

I realize that my sisters and I have a close relationship. We love and care about each other. My sisters have a habit of going to great lengths, traveling great distances, and giving up their days-off when I need them. With loving care boxes are opened, their contents unwrapped. But, you've got to know that unpacking boxes and unwrapping "things" is not all that occurs when my sisters come. Laughter, conversation, and memory fill what has been empty space. From different areas of the house, we converge repeatedly to share family history, to recall significant people, and to connect again with our ancestors. For as the oldest child, the Big Sister, I am the keeper of many heirlooms and treasures. I hold our collective story in quilts, dishes, photographs, and whatnots from days gone by. We unpack our individual pain with each other.

We release hurt that others have heaped upon us. We let go of anger that has been simmering for too long. We shed the masks we're forced to wear in public to maintain professional fronts. We unwrap our hopes for ourselves and our families. We are gentle with each other as layers of dead dreams are thrown out with the trash. When sisters gather, it's also a time to clean out useless junk!

Everything we possess is not essential! We carry too much from place to place, locked away in the "trunk" of our memory. However, many treasures are uncovered, unearthed, and discovered in a move. Often good "stuff" has been pushed under crawl spaces, neglected, and forgotten. But, when the sisters come, all things are open to scrutiny, question, and challenge. Some things are received, as gifts, by another sister. Some things are taken to the younger set of our children to help them establish their own homes. Some things are determined "useless" and tossed away or relegated to cleaning rags. But, everything is up for inspection.

When my sisters came this time, as usual, they spent only one night with me. They didn't come to stay! We ate home-cooked meals and even got in a minor shopping trip while they were here. We talked about each other. We laughed with each other. We pressed sensitive issues; probed delicate spots and pried into one another's business without apology. We listened to old-fashioned church music and evoked the spirits of our foreparents, who joined us while we did the "holy dance." We delighted ourselves in the precious gift of time together, working and creating beauty.

Around midnight, we turned off the light, adjusted the chandelier, and sat, enjoying the fruit of our labors. Things were in place. The house was in order. Tranquillity reigned. Everything looked magnificent. It was then that Baby Sister said, "Linda, I'm going to buy a new house. And, I'm going to make sure that when we move, it will be a time that you are in the country and able to come and help me." All she has to do is call. The sisters will gather!

This second volume of *Sister to Sister* is a gathering of the sisters! We've each "moved" since the first volume was released as a blessing to the sisterhood. I kept my copy close at hand in a parsonage in Chicago as I wrestled with a complex group of people and issues. It was both helpful and healthful to glean insights from other sisters who knew my struggle. But, I've moved twice since then! I'm in a "new place," geographically, vocationally, spiritually, and emotionally. I have new responsibilities with another set of complex people and issues. So, like you, I need the sisters to gather again.

This opportunity to gather a select group of my sisters is a gift from God. I offer thankful praise for this special set of women from around the country, who have been healing links in my circle of life. I've been touched by the balm of their lives, inspired by their witness, and encouraged by their collective wisdom. My prayer has been and continues to be that the healing

God will provide a double anointing to every hand used to assemble this divine medicine chest called *Sister to Sister, Volume 2*!

It's my pleasure to announce that *there is a balm in Gilead*! God has called. And the sisters have gathered! Healing is in order. Help is available. The prescription is "Take when needed." Expect to be made better. Anticipate wholeness. Pass the blessings on to others. Go on now, gather the sisters!

Shalom,

Sista Linda H. Hollies
Editor

Editor's Note about Scripture

I take great personal liberty with Scripture! I believe the Bible was written for men and women both, and I know it needs to have inclusive language to include all of us. So in editing this work, I have attempted to be true to the sources of every scriptural reference. However, some Bible versions are not wholly inclusive in their language. Therefore, I pray you will be indulgent as you read your select translation and find that it does not say "exactly" what is stated on these pages. The words are what I felt was intended for the sisterhood.

Riene Adams-Morris

Self-Knowledge

I didn't know how to love myself
so I entrusted—invested—and manifested
myself to another
even though I had vowed to love only one.
The substitute accepted the forbidden me but—
somehow—in some way
he gave me not what I thought
would satisfy and complete me.
So—I was compelled to further divide myself
and give this new portion to someone else,
hoping—praying—demanding—
that his care would be better
more intense—more fulfilling—
more encompassing
than that which the other caretaker
bestowed on me.
Only—

I discovered that I had even less
of myself for me.
I found that I was more—
more empty—more longing—more seeking
for an indefinable something.
Something that couldn't be found in
other arms—other places—other situations.
I came to know that
adultery can only be avoided
If—
I first love my God enough
to be taught how to
save myself—interest myself—
respect myself—improve myself
for my God and myself, first and foremost!
Only then can someone else come
and enjoy me with my whole precious self
in complete attendance.

**Thought for the Day: Self-knowledge
comes when the Sisters gather.**

Riene Adams-Morris is a poet, evangelist, and member of Liberty Temple Church of God in Christ in Gary, Indiana. She teaches in the Gary Public School system and is a program counselor specializing in forward movement of the mentally and physically challenged. She is mother of two sons and a grandmother.

Paulette Handley Ajavon

Freeze!

Those who wait for the Lord shall renew their strength. —Isaiah 40:31 *(NRSV)*

A favorite game of childhood is playing "Freeze." In case you don't remember, that's the game where you run, jump, skip, hop, or move however you so choose until the leader of the game yells, "Freeze!" You then cease all motion as if you were frozen in place. You remain still until you are told to move again. Teachers continue to use this game when they really need to get students' attention so that they can be given important information.

As adults, we still use the concepts of the game in our lives, especially in our relationships with God. We're quick to say, "Wait for the Lord!" meaning "Freeze!" Unfortunately, sometimes we lose the sense of purpose for "freezing" our action. We act as though waiting on the Lord means we have no responsibility, that we can just shut down as though we expect the Lord to do a magic act in our lives rather than to act with marvelously divine intervention.

Waiting is an action term. It is a faith term. To wait means to "freeze" action until the expected outcome takes place. To wait for the Lord means to be attentive as you are waiting for the Lord's direction on how to handle matters. For impatient people such as myself, waiting on the Lord often means delaying gratification until the right time—the Lord's time.

I remember when I was looking for a house to buy. I became very impatient. I knew that God had opened doors so that I could be blessed with a home of my own, but I wanted to make every house the right house. I started to see potential in even the most broken-down shacks. Yet, none of these houses "felt" right. How could these houses be "mine" when I had no spouse to be the "handyman," little or no carpentry skills, and most certainly not an endless bank account to pay for renovations or numerous repairs? So I waited and continued to search and pray over the matter.

A few weeks later I visited a friend who told me about a house around the corner from her that had been relocated and placed on a new foundation, given all new wiring, new fixtures, new plumbing, a new garage, and a built-in kitchen. This was the answer to my many prayers, which had begun a long time ago! When I looked in the window, that house called my name! I knew it was the right place for me. Today, it is my awesomely beautiful home! God has more than answered my prayers; the Lord blessed and renewed me that, as part of my ministry, I might be a blessing to others by assisting them with home ownership.

To wait for the Lord is to live out our faith! To wait for the Lord means to seek daily the guidance of the Holy Spirit. Most importantly, to wait for the Lord means to believe in God's promises to never leave us or forsake us. When we "freeze" our actions, our processes, and our attempts to "fix it," we allow the divine action of the Holy Spirit to inform, transform, and renew our strength and our relationships with God and with others.

Thought for the Day: Lord, yell "Freeze!" because I await your voice. Renew my strength daily so that I may

do your will. Continue to bless me, Lord, so that I may be a blessing to others.

Paulette Handley Ajavon is the founder and executive director of Colorful Threads Inc.: Weaving Together Strands of Wholeness, a Minnesota nonprofit agency. She is also director of Project SPIRIT and the associate pastor of Camphor United Methodist Church. She earned both her B.A. and M.A. from Webster University and her M.Div. from Eden Theological Seminary.

Maude A. Alexander

Who Is God?

God is spirit, and those who worship
God must worship in spirit and in truth.
—John 4:24 (NRSV)

"Grandma, who is God?" My four-year-old grandson asked me this question of primary essence the morning after I told him not to worry about his ailing mother. I told him that God would make her better. And from his ever inquisitive mind came life's most important question—and I was not prepared to give him that all important answer. Thank God he did not want a weighty answer nor was he ready for it. He simply said "Oh" when I said that God is that One who made us, who wants us to be good and to help each other.

Who is God? My grandmother, who worked in white folks' kitchens most of her adult life, would say, "God is my All in All." My father, who labored as a custodian for our local electric company for twenty-seven years, would say in his quiet way, "God is the Lily of the Valley." My mother would identify God as she ironed and sang "Precious Lord." She seldom made any distinction between God and Jesus Christ. My oldest son, an electrical engineer, encountered God in a closet when he was four years old and said, "God is the Wheel in the middle of a wheel."

My brother who is a minister would say, "God is the great I AM; God is love; God is omnipresent and omnipotent." My pastor has described God in many realities, but for me, his most memorable description is that "God is inclusive," emphasizing that the Almighty does not discriminate against any human regardless of race, sex, criminal record, size, state of mind, et cetera. God is concerned about all human beings—yes, even about all of nature.

My oldest daughter knows God in the essence of omnipresence. My younger daughter knows God as Love, enduring. My sisters know God as Comforter and Healer. My younger son sees God revealed through the beauty and challenges offered by two very young children.

And I know God through all the relationships I have—with those named above and with others. God has been my sustainer through forty-two years of marriage and parenthood, to my children from their infancy through their experiences in college, the corporate world, and now their own families.

To me, God is a merciful, personal reality. My greatest challenge will be to guide my grandchildren into understanding through their own personal relationship with God, the Creator. Who is God to you?

Thought for the Day: God is a spirit who is our all and all.

Maude A. Alexander is a retired educator, early childhood and cultural diversity consultant, poet, and folk artist. She is chaplain of the Louisville Section of the National Council of Negro Women and member of the St. Stephen Baptist Church, Louisville, Kentucky.

Lula Bailey Ballton

Burned Out!

*The servant of the Lord won't break
off a bent reed or put out a dying flame,
but will make sure that justice is done.*
—Isaiah 42:3 (CEV)

At the kitchen table my friend poured out her
heart and told of another relational disappointment. "I'm so tired of men who lie, cheat, and
deceive. *I'm burnt out.* My daughter and my
career are my only interests from now on."

Another sister-friend at the table chimed in,
"Not only men, but people on my job are the
same way." She told of the many times she covered for her boss, the times she worked late
without overtime pay, the extras she provided,
and the years dedicated to the company in
general and her boss in particular. He praised
her but did not pay her. After seven years he

received a big promotion and raise. She received a good-bye bouquet when he hired a new, younger assistant who was not black. "No more," she continued, "no more unappreciated sacrifices, no more long hours and low pay. *I am burning. I was burnt, and now I am burned out!*"

The table conversation continued as we shared scorching tales of the infidelity of friends and disappointments in our lives. The flames of it all seemed to lick the pink Formica top on the old kitchen table. Then suddenly we were awash with a quiet—one of those silences that is filled with expectation.

Slowly and one by one we started to giggle. Giggle as only "the girls" do when the relief of survival bursts forth. Giggles turned to outright laughter until a new out-of-breath contented quiet emerged. The quiet of consensus.

"You know what," I shared, "through it all I learned to trust in Jesus. I learned to call his name. I know that it is Jesus Christ who is keeping me from giving up and burning out."

Isn't it just like our Lord to remind us that nothing can separate us from God's love—just when we need it most?

We had come together thinking we were *burnt out*. Jesus Christ reminded us in our sistership that, if we were bent over, he would not let us break, and if we were the candle wick flickering, *he would not let our fire burn out.*

Thank you, Lord, for bringing us through. Thank you for making us survivors. We appreciate the *fire wall* of your love.

Thought for the Day: Christ's love is a fire wall for today's disappointments.

Lula Bailey Ballton, co-founder and executive director of the West Angeles Community Corporation in Los Angeles, California, is a lawyer, educator, writer, and a licensed missionary in the Church of God in Christ. She earned an M.A. in communications from Northwestern University and her J.D. from UCLA School of Law.

Helen Davis Bell

When Forgiveness Is Hard

. . . and be kind to one another, tenderhearted, forgiving one another, as God in Christ has forgiven you.
—*Ephesians 4:32* (RSV)

After the 1954 Supreme Court decision, *Brown vs. The Board of Education,* I was one of seven black twelve- and thirteen-year-old students to pilot school integration in an all-white school in Charleston, West Virginia. It was a difficult year—one filled with much fear and anxiety.

There was one teacher, however, who was very special. When not in class, I spent a number of hours sharing with her, discussing my hopes and dreams, my concerns and my fears. She offered encouragement, advice, and friendship. Most importantly, I believed she cared for me. The color of my skin was not a barrier to our relationship.

One day while on my way to class, another black student and I overheard this teacher telling a joke about a "nigger in the woodshed." They both were doubled over in laughter which only ended when they realized that we were standing there and had heard the whole exchange. I was deeply hurt and disappointed. I remember later saying to my father, "I not only trusted her, but I liked her." Despite the fact that she later apologized for her behavior, I had decided that I hated her and would never trust a white person again.

My father explained to me the importance of forgiveness. He said there would be many persons during my lifetime who would disappoint and hurt me, who would not live up to my expectations, but that God expects us to manifest the same spirit of forgiveness toward others that God has shown toward us. He told me that carrying unforgiveness and hatred in my heart denies me the possibility of being the whole person God intended me to be.

I would like to be able to say that I accepted what he said and appropriated it right away. But,

I needed some time to work through those feelings. Eventually, I was able to forgive both teachers. I have learned over the years that my father was right. Forgiveness is something we all have to struggle with many times during a lifetime. It is not easy. Many of us have experienced failed marriages, children who have disappointed us, people on our jobs, in our communities, our churches who are a constant source of friction and frustration. People make mistakes, and for this reason ill-treatment of self and others is simply one of the facts with which all of us must deal.

In the Gospel of Matthew, Peter asked Jesus how many times a person should forgive (Matthew 18:21–22). Jesus answered Peter with a story set in the context of God's grace, a story about a king, a servant, and a debt. The point that Jesus made was that our debt to God is totally and forever beyond the possibility of payment. Therefore, God's forgiveness reveals God's immeasurable grace.

What does God's forgiveness demand of us? It insists that we look at each other through the eyes of mercy. Forgiveness is a right relationship with both God and our neighbor. Forgiveness means that one is able to love genuinely, with a love that goes beyond the problem and extends to the person(s) involved.

A young girl said it best. When asked to define forgiveness, she answered, "It is the odor that flowers breathe when they are trampled on." True forgiveness looks beyond what an individual does to us. True forgiveness once concluded, "They know not what they do."

Thought for the Day: To refuse to forgive enables the past, with its errors and mistakes, to sit in on the present as a constant troublemaker.

Helen Davis Bell, a graduate of West Virginia State College, received her M.Div. from Gammon Theological Seminary, the Interdenominational Theological Center in Atlanta, Georgia. She is an ordained clergywoman of the Tennessee Annual Conference of the United Methodist Church, where she currently serves as the pastor of Seay-Hubbard United Methodist Church in Nashville, Tennessee. She is a mother and grandmother.

Cynthia B. Belt

It Is Well with My Soul

*For I consider that our present suf-
ferings are not worth comparing with
the glory that will be revealed in us.*
—Romans 8:18 (NIV)

The song "It Is Well" is one of my favorites.
When I am most troubled, this is the song that
rings in my spirit. When I am most elated, this
song rings in my spirit. It is my testimony and
my witness. It is well with my soul. No matter
what goes on in my life, no matter how hard the
trials, no matter what the difficulties, I can stand
and declare that *it is well with my soul*! My soul
is in the hands of my God, and I shall never be
plucked from the Lord's hands. My eternity is
secure.

In one setting I was asked, "How can this song have any real meaning for you as an African American female? You have been so oppressed and so rejected—even in the church—that it must be impossible for you to believe in all this stuff!" My response was that despite all the negative things that have happened around me, despite all of the trials and tribulations, despite all of the oppression and despair, I can rejoice in the assurance that it is well with my soul. I remember my ancestors who came here in chains and heard something in the gospel message that resonated with their souls. Their deep connection was to Jesus Christ, and they understood that God would indeed free them from bondage.

Romans 8:18 tells us that the sufferings of this present world are not worthy to be compared to the glory that God has in store for us. Every now and then I get glimpses of that glory. I've seen it in the neonatal intensive care unit as seriously ill babies are nursed to health and in the eyes of the street person who promises to keep watch until I get to my car in a rough neighborhood. I've seen God's glory in the eyes of an elderly mother who knows her Savior and is not afraid to die and in the being of a young man who was dying, knowing that his eternity was sure in Jesus Christ. I've seen God's glory in the life of a friend who has dedicated her life to service among the poor and outcast. These glimpses of eternity make me grateful, and thankful that *it is well with my soul*.

I am strengthened by our foremothers who were bound in body, but free in their spirits, who stood strong in their spirits and lived despite the degradation of slavery as they embraced the gospel of Jesus Christ. They did not hear in the gospel a message of passive acceptance, but they heard a call to give their allegiance to Jesus Christ, their true master, the one who had the power to raise them up above their circumstances. Because of their example, I can stand against oppression, degradation, and evil and declare that *it is well with my soul*.

I think of Harriet Tubman, who heard in the gospel message a call to rise and leave the house of bondage but also to go back and lead her brothers and sisters to deliverance. I recall Sojourner Truth who heard in the gospel message a call to stand against racism and sexism, by declaring before a convention of Anglo women and men, "Ain't I a woman?" I remember both Ida Wells and Mary Church Terrill, who heard in the gospel message a call to use their

God-given gifts and their connections to write and speak about the atrocities of the South. I am reminded of Mary McLeod Bethune, who heard in the gospel message a call to rise and educate her people. I recollect the lives of Jarena Lee and Julia Foote, who answered God's call to rise up and preach the Gospel of Jesus Christ. These were called "daughters of thunder," sisters who rose up and said by their lives, "God does not have a respect of gender! God called me to preach the Word."

I thank God for contemporary sisters like Mother Rosa Parks, Shirley Chisholm, and Barbara Jordan and all the other daughters of God who have stood up because they heard God's call to rise and motivate their people to action. With these women, I can stand boldly because *it is well with my soul.*

Thought for the Day: God, I thank you that amidst elation and despair, triumph and defeat, sickness and health, life and death—*it is well with my soul.* Lord, in whatever circumstances I find myself, let me rest in the knowledge that you have my life firmly held in your hands and that you will not let me go. Amen.

Cynthia B. Belt is a member of the Baltimore-Washington Annual Conference and the pastor of Mt. Tabor United Methodist Church. She graduated summa cum laude with an M.Div. from Wesley Theological Seminary. She is a wife and mother who is continuing her formal education by working on her doctorate.

Brigitte A. Black

Stand Up for What Is Rightfully Yours!

Therefore put on the full armor of God, so that when the day of evil comes, you may be able to stand your ground, and after you have done everything, to stand. —Ephesians 6:13 (NIV)

Recently, a sister celebrated one year of freedom from an abusive relationship. She sat in the middle of the floor and cried. Her child encouraged her not to cry for the abusive husband because he had not treated her right. Another sister took a stance by attending group therapy against domestic violence and strengthening her resolve to never again become involved in a violent relationship. She made a conscious decision to learn the destructive

22

patterns that kept her involved in violent relationships.

The enemy of our soul and the host of demonic forces have tried to hold us back and hold us down. Now is the time, as we approach the twenty-first century, to stand up for what is rightfully ours. Safety and security are ours if we stand. Joy and justice are ours if we stand. Healing and wholeness are ours if we stand. Peace of mind is ours if we stand. We have to stand against the tricks, schemes, and plots of the enemy, or we will be victims to the vicissitudes and hostages to the horrors of this life. God's Word instructs us "to stand your ground, and after you have done everything, to stand" (Ephesians 6:13).

All too often we allow the majority culture to dictate our behaviors and the opinion of others to define our actions. "Don't make waves. Go along to get along. You are shooting yourself in the foot. You are acting uppity," and on and on. These are ways of keeping us from standing up for what is rightfully ours.

Therefore, sisters, African American women, royal queens, God's sun-kissed daughters—let's take a stand for what is rightfully ours! Stand up for our God-given rights. Every promise in

God's Word is for us. We are joint heirs to every promise of God. And we know that the Word of God is true and will not fail.

Consider the story in Numbers 27:1–11 where five courageous women stood up for what was rightfully theirs, and as a result, the law was rewritten. Never before in Israel had women taken such a stand. No legal precedent existed for the five daughters of Zelophehad to come and plead their case before Moses, Eleazar the priest, and the leaders of the congregation. These women explained that their father had been faithful to God, but since he did not have any male children, they argued that they should inherit the land. Moses took their case before God. The Lord God Almighty declared the sisters were right, that they should receive their father's inheritance. Because they took the initiative and made a stand, the law was changed—not only for them but for their daughters and granddaughters in generations to come—so that daughters could inherit if a man had no sons.

Sisters, stand up for what is rightfully yours, and God will swiftly vindicate and bring justice.

Thought for the Day: The Bible contains the promises of God. Therefore, stand on the promises and receive the blessings of God.

Brigitte A. Black, an ordained elder in the African Methodist Episcopal Church, pastors Coppin Chapel African Methodist Episcopal Church in Indianapolis, Indiana. She is a dramatist, as well as a field education supervisor at Christian Theological Seminary, where she is currently working on her D.Min. in pastoral care and counseling.

Valerie Bridgeman Davis

Present in the Hard Times

Rejoice with those who rejoice; mourn with those who mourn. —*Romans 12:15 (NIV)*

I was stunned. I had just surprised my friend with a "passing through your area" visit the weekend before. An athletic woman in very good health, my forty-plus friend was extremely beautiful late in her pregnancy. Though she looked tired, there was nothing to warn either of us of the soon-coming grief. A week later, stunned and saddened, I was riding in a limousine, sitting next to my friend and her husband as we prepared to bury their daughter, born and dead too soon.

I had hustled to find the funds to get back to Alabama. I knew that there would be no words

I could say, no thing I could do, that would lessen the shock and the sharp pain in their hearts. They had waited almost twenty years of marriage for this daughter, who was named after my girlfriend's grandmothers. But this long-awaited daughter was already gone, and the empty nursery—decorated with the keen eye for creativity, history, and detail that inhabits my friend's entire home—was a painful testimony to the emptiness we were all feeling in that car. Words seemed disingenuous. Gifts seemed hopelessly banal. Even my presence there seemed frivolous to me in the presence of such profound sorrow. But these were my friends of twenty-six years and the godparents to my college-bound son. There was no where elsc I would be when they were experiencing such loss. I knew that, just as I had planned to rejoice with them and revel in being "Auntie Val," I now had to mourn with them.

I have purposed to be with them through the grieving process. Others have gone back to their lives; "our" baby's death was only a brief interlude in otherwise hectic lives. But for my friends, life will always be marked from this event. It takes time to navigate the grief, sorrow, and loss—months, years, even decades. And though others' sorrow is perhaps the most uncomfortable emotion for many of us to face, it is precisely in these times of tragedy and grief that friends need us for the long haul. The hollow space can never be filled, but perhaps as a faithful companion, I can help hallow this space.

It's tough work, grief. It's gritty and messy, and just when your emotions seem under control, something triggers the sorrow afresh, like an accidental bump can rip the scab off a wound. I can never feel as deeply or as profoundly my friends' loss. But I will continue to walk with them as long as it takes to find a fruitful land on the other side of this, the valley of the shadow of death.

Thought for the Day: May God give strength for the hard journeys and friends all along the way.

Valerie Bridgeman Davis has more than twenty years in the preaching ministry and is executive pastor of Banah Full Community Church, Austin, Texas. She also teaches religion courses at Huston-Tillitson College and has extensive experience in grief, loss, and crisis intervention through serving as a contract chaplain for Hospice Austin. Valerie, a wife, mother, and sister-friend, holds an M.Div. and is completing a Ph.D. in biblical studies at Baylor University.

Vivian C. Bryant

Resting in the Lord

All our steps are ordered by the Lord!
—Proverbs 20:24 (NRSV)

Everybody is tired. Tired emotionally. Tired intellectually. Tired physically. Tired spiritually. Tired psychologically. Tired! Tired! Tired! If we are not careful, some of us will find ourselves dead tired!

But, the question is, what is a human being to do—especially, what is a *female* human being to do? Women are called upon to be nice, be friendly, be kind, be positive, be reliable, be dependable, be super-human, be altruistic; to solve problems, mend hurts, assist others, work hard, deny self, give time, give talent, give interests; to share everything, request nothing, work miracles, display faith, show hope—and never complain of being tired!

With folks pulling and pushing, stomping and screaming, demanding and needing—women are tired! Yet, the Word of God tells us, "All our steps are ordered by the Lord; how then can we understand our own way?" (Proverbs 20:24 NRSV). In other words, it is a waste of time to worry simply because we can not comprehend everything if God is in charge of our life.

Yet the question remains: how can we experience rest in a tired world, surrounded by tired people, while surviving in a tired society, encountering tired conditions, produced by tired circumstances?

The answer is by learning how to rest in the Lord. This rest means freedom from anxiety. It implies peace in spite of what is going on in life. It embraces a confidence in knowing that God is in charge. God is in control! So, we do not have to personally deal with every challenge of the moment! We can defer every assignment to a God who is ready, willing, and able to handle whatever comes our way.

Think of a small, obedient child, holding on to her mother's hand, allowing her mother to lead the way. The child does not resist being led. The child does not adopt an interrogative mode, questioning the mother concerning motivation nor destination. The child simply keeps her hand in her mother's hand, walking in confidence that Mommy knows the way.

We, too, need to place our very lives in God's hand. We can learn to allow God to lead and direct us. We can allow God to order our steps. We need to have confidence that God really does know where we need to go, how to get us there, and when we need to arrive at the desired destination. We can stop being tired! We have no need nor excuse to be tired any longer! Let God be the director of your life.

Thought for the Day: If the Lord delights in a woman's way, God will make her steps firm; though she stumble, she will not fall, for the Lord upholds her with a divine hand (Psalm 37:23 NIV).

Vivian C. Bryant, an ordained elder, serves as one of the pastors on staff at Hope United Methodist Church in Southfield, Michigan. She has been awarded Teacher of the Year status for her diligence and love for teaching. She is married to William R. Bryant and has a daughter, Darmetta, and a son, William Junior.

E. Anne Henning Byfield

Today May Be a Divine Setup

*You must stay calm and be willing
to suffer. You must work hard to tell
the good news and to do your job well.*
—2 Timothy 4:5 (CEV)

Several years ago I was asked to preach at a
major event. Never before had a woman been
invited to speak there. My choir rehearsed for
weeks. My family flew in, and the place was
packed. When the sermon was over, the people
went into shouts of celebration.

When the benediction was pronounced, my
family and the women all rushed to me. There
were tears, hugs, and handshaking. My mother
had her own greeting line. I noticed that only a
few brothers shook my hand. Outside waiting

was a small group of preachers. Their questions were fast and angry: "Why did you use this moment to raise women's issues? Why did you preach on Huldah? Why did you destroy the preaching moment?" I responded that neither Huldah nor women were the focus of the text.

In my room, a friend asked me the same questions. I threw the manuscript on the table and told him to read it. He realized there were only four paragraphs referring to women and they were germane to the pericope. As he read it, he got very quiet, said he was sorry, and walked out.

What should have been an affirming night ended in pain. As I prayed—no, as I *complained*, I was moved to call a mentor. After pouring out my anguish, he responded angrily, "What did you think was going to happen? You were the first woman to preach in one hundred fifty years. Besides, who else is going to preach the woman's message? Get over it! Go to sleep! And praise God that you were an available vessel."

Was this a divine setup? A divine setup is when our mission is one issue and God has another agenda in mind. You get up to respond to a question at a Bible study and end up sharing that you are an abuse/incest survivor.

God takes the opportunity with people who are willing to do what needs to be done even when the task looks silly, foolish, or impossible. Then God uses you to accomplish God's will for you and others.

So, get over the jeers. Listen if you have a need. Don't listen if you don't have a desire. For today, you are doing what you are supposed to do! Create! Renew! Reform! Celebrate! Laugh! And, rejoice even in the tears! God is in control.

Thought for the Day: Lord, help me to be available and sensitive to your agenda. Set me up today to accomplish your purposes!

E. Anne Henning Byfield is pastor of Robinson Community AME Church in Indianapolis, Indiana, where she has a particular focus on the healing of the African American family. She has an undergraduate degree from Wilberforce University and did her graduate work at Christian Theological Seminary. She is a third generation preacher, married to Ainsley with one son, Michael.

Carolyn A. H. Campbell

A Quiet Spirit

> *For I am longing to see you so that I may share with you some spiritual gift to strengthen you—or rather so that we may be mutually encouraged by each other's faith, both yours and mine.*
> *—Romans 1:11–12 (NRSV)*

I have limited use for labels or titles—both seem to cause people to be immediately placed in a predetermined category or "box." Yet I found myself participating in the very same thought processes that I have felt were limiting me.

My faith journey has offered me a variety of experiences across denominational lines. I have envied my sisters in Christ who could quote scripture word for word, chapter and verse. I desperately wanted to be able to pray the prayers of saints past and present with fervor. I wanted to sing like an angel. I wanted to bellow out my testimony while dancing in the spirit. I wanted to be affirmed with hardy *amens*. I wanted to be able to speak in tongues as hands were laid on those who approached the altar for anointing and prayer. But what I wanted was not what God wanted for me.

My role in life seemed to be "the watcher." I would evaluate the circumstances and decide if the consequences or rewards warranted my participation. If my siblings or peers participated in an activity that brought about punishment, I would not venture out to try the same thing— unless rebellion set in. If an activity brought about too much attention to the participants, I would not join them because of my introverted nature. Eventually I found myself not doing much of anything and being mired in a state of depression.

At the crossroads of rejection and silence, I sought understanding and I could only turn to God. My friends could not and did not want to understand what was happening with me. Like Job I was told I "had sinned" and that God was using depression as a way to call me to repentance. In my heart of hearts I knew those friends were wrong. Like Elijah fleeing from the threat of death, I retreated into a dismal cave only to be stirred by the still, small voice on the winds.

My days of struggle in "sackcloth and ashes" were long, but I knew I had not been forsaken. Daily the words "be still, and know that I am God" (Psalm 46:10 NRSV) kept me from buying into self-pity or the predetermined diagnosis of my "friends" who assumed I was in a spiritual war of my own creation. The tender touches, smiles, kisses, and presence of a loving and persistent family and of vintage practitioners (wise saints), along with the assistance of a physician and psychologist, enabled me to take the threads of my life and knit them back together. The presence of my sisters in Christ was noticeably absent.

As God always does, God used this experience to grant me greater self-awareness. While in the midst of turmoil, I began to see the silent struggle of others. One by one, families began to acknowledge their experiences with depression. Their mild to tragic stories strengthened me—for then I accepted that I was not alone. As I experienced release from depression, my victory became one of the vehicles that transported and transformed the healing process of others.

My "horror" opened the doors of conversation. One friend shared that she thought she would never understand the complexity of depression, but because we valued our friendship, we worked hard to maintain the relationship God had established. In spite of ourselves and our differing opinions, that friendship grew even deeper—and remains solid to this day. She now has a ministry with younger women traveling down the same road—if not worse.

As things returned to "normal," whispers continued, but I was determined not to let the whisperers stop me. I had greater determination, and I knew God had a call on my life. On an April morning during Sunday worship, the answer came. My eyes fell upon Romans 1:10–16, and I began to shout, dance, and pray prayers of thanksgiving. Several people remarked, "I didn't know you spoke in tongues!" I responded, "I don't! God allowed me to experience that which I desired!" That outward manifestation was only for a season, but on that day God affirmed my quiet spirit as a gift. I no longer envy any other sister's gifts and abilities. I have come to realize and to appreciate that God has given me this quiet spirit!

Years after that April revelation, a colleague presented me with a book. In it she inscribed, "To my quiet, radical friend who walks in quiet ways and tends to unspoken needs—may God continue to use you as an instrument to bring about change."

Thought for the Day: Some of us gather our gifts slowly along the way, and when we ponder what took so long, we realize the treasures we hold in our baskets were created like fine black pearls.

Carolyn A. H. Campbell, an administrative assistant in admissions and student life, is currently pursuing her M.A. in the women's studies in theology, religion, and ministry program at United Theological Seminary of the Twin Cities of New Brighton, Minnesota. She is a certified lay speaker in the Minnesota Annual Conference of the United Methodist Church and co-facilitator of the Women's Ministry Initiative at Camphor Memorial UMC in St. Paul, Minnesota, where her husband, Rufus, is pastor.

Lillian Harris Carter

Shun Fear!

> *For the waywardness of the simple will kill them, and the complacency of fools will destroy them; but whoever listens to wisdom will live in safety, and be at ease, without fear of harm.*
> *—Proverbs 1:32–33 (NIV)*

Fear is such a powerful emotion that it affects us physically and mentally. We fear our neighborhood ills—the drugs, violence, crime. We fear our supervisors on the job. We fear closed spaces and open waters. We fear traveling over bridges or riding in elevators. As a matter of fact, those things that we fear could be as numerous as the people you question about it!

Fear paralyzes us. It causes us to perspire profusely, to become dry-mouthed, to have butterflies in our stomachs. It keeps us from speaking fluently and assuredly, making us stammer and lose our voices. Fear keeps us in our homes, looking out rather than going out. It makes us paranoid about our coworkers and friends. We distrust family members and neighbors as well as strangers.

Fear is so pervasive and overwhelming that we can become sick because of it. But these extremes only happen when we do not claim the saving grace and the magnificent mercy of our Lord and Savior, Jesus Christ.

In Psalm 27:1, David reminds us: "The Lord is my light and salvation—whom shall I fear?" This statement can and should be taken literally because when you walk with the assurance that the Lord *is* your light and salvation, then you need to fear *no thing* and *no one*. God places sweet peace and quietness within our reach. I'm a witness that our God soothes our anxieties, calms our mistrusts, settles our upsets. Our God is all-powerful.

Even before we carry all that concerns us to the throne of grace, we can claim the victory! As we share in prayer our concerns, our troubles, and our fears, God delights to provide the inner assurance that will allow us to move to the next task. Once I make the decision to turn my fears over to the One who calms the storms, I begin to question why I waited so long to resort to this tried and true solution, which is so simple.

Our God is serenity. The Maker of heaven and earth is the very essence of calm in the midst of the storm. Our Sovereign Lord is peace in wartime and relief in distress. God is all that you need. Fearful? I'm a witness that God is more than able to give you sweet rest.

Thought for the Day: Do not fear! God is in charge!

Lillian Harris Carter is a divorced mother of two adult sons, whom she loves, and the nurturer of over 2,000 former students, whom she knows "by heart." She has been teaching in the public schools of Richmond, Virginia, for twenty-five years.

Janette E. Chandler-Kotey

A Lost Opportunity to Pray

> *If my people, which are called by my name, shall humble themselves, and pray, and seek my face, and turn from their wicked ways; then will I hear from heaven, and will forgive their sin, and will heal their land. —2 Chronicles 7:14 (KJV)*

African American women have a strong nurturing side that causes us to take ownership of the brokenness and hurt we see, whatever the situation: from a sick child to a drug-dependent child, from no husband to an unfaithful husband, from a bad friend to a friend in a bad relationship, from a sister hesitant to respond to the call on her life because of fear of rejection

43

to a sister who doesn't know who she is or where she wants to go. I know from personal experience that sometimes this nurturing side is out of balance with the will of God. Often I see a problem before I know how to respond to the problem. In my own power I set out to fix what I do not even fully understand. Then I find myself in a real complex mess!

I have had to learn that God does not show me the sin or weakness of others so that I can assume the place of their Messiah. I have come to realize that I am only to pray the will of God for others' lives so they can see God as their source—not me.

From the beginning of time, humans have conformed to the ways of the world as opposed to being transformed to the will and way of God. We are continually faced with all sorts of sickness in our land. We experience bad marriages, dysfunctional families, rebellious children, and even sinfully sick national and religious leaders. And, when as people of God, we become so satisfied, so complacent that we do not pray and do not speak out but accept the sins of the world because those sins are the norm, then we participate in the causes of destruction in the land.

Our human need to expose, judge, and punish can cause us to miss opportunities to bring about healing that will affect the perpetrator, the victim, ourselves, and our communities. These are not opportunities to build up our egos by finding others with greater faults than our own! Finding "worse sinners" has always been easy. But, 2 Chronicles 7:14 tells us what we should do when we confront sinful behaviors in ourselves and others.

All of life provides us with opportunities to intercede on behalf of those who are straying from the will of God. Our spiritual nature should remind us that the battle is not ours. Whatever the situation may be, it belongs to the Lord! For God is God all alone. We have to refrain from judging and from taking ownership! What we do affects the lives of others. How we respond to what others do affects our own lives. If we judge, we will be judged. However, if we learn to pray and turn away from labeling and judging, we will be healed. The sin-sick will be healed. And our nation will be healed.

Only God can work the healing. We are called to intercede and be the go-betweens. Prayer conforms us to God's will. This is the reason that we pray! So, sisters, pray, remembering that prayer really does change things—and that the first thing prayer changes is we who are praying!

Thought for the Day: Lord, help me to pray and trust you to work out the details.

Janette E. Chandler-Kotey is the pastor of music and the arts at St. Paul United Methodist Church in Dallas, Texas. She earned her M.Div. at Oral Roberts University in Tulsa, Oklahoma, where she is completing her doctorate. She is a wife and the mother of three daughters.

Michelle A. Cobb

A True Presence

Even though I walk through the valley of the shadow of death, I will fear no evil. . . . —Psalm 23:4 (NIV)

A very familiar line from a very comforting psalm. Have you ever walked through the "valley of the shadow of death"?

What was your personal valley? Was it one of illness, financial ruin, family strain? Were you caught off guard by the shadows you found there?

My mother had been critically ill for several months before I came to the realization that I was walking in my very own "valley of the shadow of death." This valley was unfamiliar to me because it had bends and turns to which I was unaccustomed. I had traveled through other "valleys," but this "valley" journey was more intense; the route was more treacherous.

I'm not sure why I was caught off guard by the bend that led to the shadows of despair and dread. But I was. I'm not sure why I was caught off guard by the turns that confronted me with the domineering stance and intimidating presence of fear. But I was.

Could it be that this valley appeared to be more treacherous because I had detoured onto the road with some preconceived ideas of how God would be with me?

"Even though I walk through the valley of the shadow of death, I will fear no evil, for you are with me; your rod and your staff, they comfort me" (Psalm 23:4).

Yes! Throughout my valley journey, the Lord was with me—not as I had perceived that God would be, but as the Lord knew I needed for God's sake and purpose for my life! I grew in that valley. I met God in a different way in that valley. I learned how to look for God to show up in forms, methods, people, occasions, and situations that were unexpected as I walked through the valley. I learned that God did not leave me alone! In the deepest part of the valley, when I did not know my way, God was there. I was never alone. God was a true presence throughout my valley travels.

Are you walking through "the valley of the shadow of death"? Look around you. Look beyond the hill of self-absorption. Look carefully. Yes, God is there—the Lord is truly present with you.

Thought for the Day: God is always with us.

Michelle A. Cobb is an elder in the United Methodist Church and pastor of the First United Methodist Church of Merriville, Indiana. She received her M.Div. from Garrett-Evangelical Theological Seminary in Evanston, Illinois. Michelle, formerly a hospital chaplain, chairs her Annual Conference's division of Racial Ethnic Local Church Ministries.

Leona J. Cochran

Hold to God's Word

I will instruct you and teach you in the way you should go; I will counsel you and watch over you. —Psalm 32:8 (NIV)

How often have you heard that "women aren't supposed" to do *this* kind of work or be in *that* kind of role? Well, I heard it often as I was growing up. So I was taken aback when God called me to ordained ministry. I had been taught that God did not use women in that role. Yet, I had a recurring dream in which God instructed me to "plant the seeds." I was confused. Was God really calling me, and for what reason?

I sought an answer to this difficult question by talking with my family, and they seemed to think I was mistaken. I talked with my friends, who shared my family's views. Each of these individuals whom I loved so much did not understand my situation. So, I talked with my pastor, who listened and suggested I go back to God for clarity. This I did!

Well, God responded by sending me to Psalm 32 and lifting up verse 8 in my mind: "I will instruct you and teach you in the way you should go; I will counsel you and watch over you." I was amazed, and yet, because of incorrect training and belief, I could not receive God's Word in its fullness. I went again to my pastor and shared this Word from God with him. He then responded with a question, "What are you going to do?"

As I reflect now upon that time in my journey with Jesus, I realize I was a babe in Christ. I felt I needed the assurance of others to interpret God's meaning to me. After much prayer and many trials, God assured me of the revelation of the divine Word in my heart. With that assurance, I stepped out on faith and trust. I had faith that God would do what God had promised! I stepped into seminary with the knowledge that the Lord would be faithful to meet every need.

Today, I can honestly say that God did far more than I could ever understand. God provided for me in ways I had not ever envisioned. God provided monies that I did not seek out. God provided me with a clear mind to learn and comprehend what I needed. God provided the Holy Spirit's anointing to change and transform me in the midst of my lack of understanding. God moved me from where I had lived with a negative spirit to a new place with a positive attitude!

As I reflect on my journey, I realize that when I asked God to do what only God could do, I had to allow the Holy Spirit to take the lead in my mind, will, and spirit. I've learned to reeducate my order of priority. Today, without a doubt, I honestly believe that "I can do all things through Christ who strengthens me" (Philippians 4:13 NKJV). And I have the experience to prove it in my life!

If you feel God's call upon your life, I encourage you to take courage and hold on to God's Word. Remember, God will give you clarity and send you forth with courage and excellence—if you believe. Don't give up on what God can do! God can do far more than any woman of God can ever imagine. In this day, God's Holy Spirit is poured out upon *all* flesh! And, my sister, that "all" includes even *you*!

Thought for the Day: "But as it is written, eye has not seen, nor ear heard, nor have entered into the heart of women, the things which God has prepared for those that love the Lord" (1 Corinthians 1:9 NKJV).

Leona J. Cochran is an ordained minister in the United Church of Christ. She is a graduate of Chicago Theological Seminary, a doctoral student, and a member of Trinity United Church of Christ in Chicago, Illinois. She is a staff chaplain at Advocate Trinity Hospital.

Alice J. Dise

What Happened after the Resurrection?

If Christ be not risen, then is our preaching in vain, and your faith is also in vain. —1 Corthinians 15:14 (KJV)

"What happened after the resurrection?" Joanna looked bewildered.

"What kind of question is that?" Tameka quipped. The two friends had attended the Passion play at Tameka's church. The teens were good friends, even though Joanna was Jewish and Tameka was an African American Christian.

The scenes connected with the trials and the crucifixion of Jesus all seemed understandable to Joanna, but she could not understand the excitement of the audience when the resurrection was re-enacted. She asked, "What happened after the resurrection?" Obviously, she wanted to know the significance of this event.

That question, "What happened after the resurrection?" if answered, would have great impact upon the lives of Joanna and countless others like her. Some folks argue that the resurrection never happened, believing the story to be nothing more than mythology. Others see it as an end in itself—having no effect on the future. Then there are those who have searched to find meaning in the resurrection and, like Paul, are convinced of its significance and implications for their future.

Paul, who at one time did not believe in the resurrection, later said, "And if Christ be not risen, then is our preaching in vain, and your faith is also in vain" (1 Corinthians 15:14). Such a statement certainly places great value upon the resurrection as it relates to the witness, beliefs, and mission of those people who would hear the story in the generations yet to come.

Mary, a woman, became a commissioned witness. The woman's call "to witness" was authenticated when *Jesus* sent her to the brethren with a message—after the resurrection.

Thomas, a doubter, became a believer. Thomas' encounter with Jesus revealed the "proofs" of the resurrection—Jesus' nail-scarred hands and side. These indeed could only belong to the crucified and resurrected Lord—after the resurrection.

The church was born. Its mission to "teach and to baptize" was given—after the resurrection.

Jesus ascended after the resurrection. He chose to "rise" in the flesh before ascending into heaven.

Death lost its sting, and the grave its victory— after the resurrection. "O death, where is thy sting? O grave, where is thy victory? But thanks be to God, which giveth us the victory through our Lord Jesus Christ" (1 Corinthians 15:55, 57 KJV).

The fact is, the faith, hopes, and dreams of countless millions have been changed forever because of the resurrection.

Thought for the Day: Be ready to answer: How has your knowledge of the resurrection affected your life and witness?

Alice J. Dise is an ordained minister of the Church of God, serving as an associate pastor and superintendent of Sunday school at the Vernon Park Church of God, Chicago. She is an editorial consultant for Urban Ministries, Inc., an African American Christian publishing company. She is a retired writer and editor of Vacation Bible School curriculum.

Rita Smith Dove

God Is Good

> *Praise the Lord, who is so good; God's love endures forever. —Psalm 136:1 (NAB)*

All over the country, in churches large and small, and even in private conversations—you need only say, "God is good, all the time," and there is an immediate refrain, "All the time, God is good." The response is automatic—even if unintentionally solicited. In worship services, it acts as a quick unifier. It's cute, catchy, and clever—a wonderful affirmation, indeed, but I often wonder if our automatic response goes any deeper. What are we thinking when we say, "God is good, all the time"? What evidence do we have that God is good? Can we say those words with absolute conviction? And if God is good all the time, what does that mean for me—day in and day out?

You will notice that the statement does not include any exceptions or disclaimers. We do not say, "God is good all the time, except when I'm at the doctor's office" or "God is good all the time, except when I am overlooked for a promotion at work" or "God is good all the time, except in eight o'clock Monday morning traffic." No exceptions are noted in terms of circumstance, time, or place. There are no exceptions noted in Psalm 136, either. In fact, "God is good" is stated throughout the Psalms. Of God's goodness, the psalmists seem convinced. Yet, knowing the life stories of these writers, it is astonishing that they testify to God's goodness . . .

in life and death,
in victory and defeat,
on the mountain or in the valley,
in plenty and in want,
in peace and war,
in love or hate,
in company or solitude,
in health or sickness,
in obedience or disobedience,
in success or failure,
in clarity or confusion,

in the miraculous and in the mundane,
in unity or discord,
in safety or danger,
in confidence or self-doubt,
in fearlessness or fear . . .
God is good, all the time! And all the
time, God is good!

Why? How? Because the love of God endures *forever*! Whenever, whatever, wherever, and forever, God's focused love and care are on us. We are never out of the sight of God's eye! God's presence is never absent. God's care is never inoperative. God constantly works on our behalf, providing redemption from sin, constant companionship, purpose for living, transformation of character, and strength and guidance for each day's journey. God is a "very present help in the time of trouble," providing daily necessities (and extras too), forgiveness, joy, hope, courage, and life eternal. Absolutely nothing can separate us from the love of God!

Indeed, God is good all the time, and all the time, God is good!

Thought for the Day: Lord, let me live my life today, knowing that you love me and that your love endures forever.

Let me know that, because you love me, you are with me every second, transforming me into the image of your Son. Fulfill your purposes in me today. Amen.

Rita Smith Dove is a graduate of Norfolk State University and Gordon Conwell Theological Seminary. She and her husband, James, now reside in Beverly, Massachusetts, where she serves as the assistant director of cooperative education and career services at a local college.

Bobbie L. Earl

Emotionally Challenged

Commit your works unto the Lord; trust in God, and the Lord will act.
—Psalm 37:5 (NRSV)

When God made woman, the world was changed forever. She brought with her sensitivity, wisdom, beauty, strength, and satisfaction (to the man). I'm proud to be part of this unique gender. However, I must admit, a part of womanhood is a bit mysterious.

Some days I'm like the Rock of Gibraltar—solid, firm, and unmovable in my stand. Then there are times I feel like crawling under the rock to seek protection from the blows of life. Sometimes I appear to have it all together, yet I can crumble in an instant when hurt or disappointed by a significant other. Sometimes I talk or listen through my tears when the subject is an issue close to my heart. What a flood of emotions!

In my quest to be more Christ-like, I often experience frustration because the emotions of "self" get in the way. We are constantly challenged to crucify this flesh and become selfless instead of selfish. That challenge can be even greater when we are in positions of leadership, when we're continually scrutinized by the public eye and perhaps attacked by critical wagging tongues. Each day brings new opportunities to practice what we preach. Sometimes I win that battle and feel a sense of accomplishment. In other instances, I seem to fail miserably, but I am determined to persevere.

I've come to realize the importance of submitting every part of myself to the Creator—even (and especially) my emotions. In doing so, I can release my own insecurities and rest in the arms of my Maker. This is not always easy, especially when I'm feeling independent and thinking, "I can handle this." Then I'm in for a rude awakening! Intelligence, wit, charm, beauty, character, and other admirable traits of womanhood are no match for the Great I AM. My ability to handle anything is closely connected with mercy and grace. I can do and be because of the Greater One who lives in me.

So, for me the mystery of womanhood—and how God works through it—remains. But that's a good thing. Mystery makes for a more interesting, exciting life that is like taking a voyage into the unknown. Most importantly, the mystery keeps me humble.

Thought for the Day: Embrace the mystery of this and every day!

Bobbie L. Earl has been an ordained minister since 1988 and currently serves in a pastoral capacity along with her husband, Anthony Earl, at Living Word International, in Chicago, Illinois. A mother, she is the founder and advisor of the Daughters of Destiny. Bobbie holds a B.S. degree in business.

Ida Elizabeth Easley

Sisters Sharing: A Matter of Choice?

If God is for us, who can be against us? —Romans 8:31 (NIV)

I grew up in the tumultuous sixties, a time of rage, anger, change, and questions of identity. As a young woman, I was like many of my sisters, wondering what it meant to be a black woman in those times. I wore an "Afro," went to meetings of the N.A.A.C.P., listened in rapt awe to the Black Panthers' ideology, and watched as Dr. Martin Luther King Jr. was jeered, cursed, and applauded. We went to Motown Revues and sang both songs of freedom and songs of love. In the midst of that scenario, I talked to my sister friends, planning to go to college and make a difference in these United

States. I had high hopes, high ideals, and high expectations. Then life happened. I went off to college, and my closest confidant and friend went to work and to play. When I returned from school without a degree, she and I began to play again together. We married, each had a child, and divorced—not quite as quickly as that sentence implies but certainly too fast! We went through the parties and the relationships of single life together. We talked and made choices that we thought were best for ourselves, at least in relation to our limited knowledge. We held on to each other and moved on. Life happened, but we continued to share those inner dreams, visions, and hopes.

Although the time came when my path went in an entirely different direction, I still hold on to the shared hopes. We as African American women need each other, whether we are doctors, lawyers, homemakers, preachers, teachers, factory workers, executives, bus drivers, or whatever else. We need to remember that our strength is in our shared pain, our shared hopes, and our shared commitment to make a positive difference. We have come through the diaspora, slavery, disenfranchisement, and the civil rights era. We have survived and often thrived. We have maintained our sanity, raised our children, loved our men, and managed our finances. We owe it to our friends, our foremothers, and ourselves to stay connected, to share, to support, and yes, even to chastise one another. Surely God has not seen us through only for us to forget from whence we came.

Thought for the Day: Why do we not value each other? Look in the mirror of a sister's eyes and see the strength and beauty; then smile, hold your head up, and praise God for the gifts we have been given.

Ida Elizabeth Easley is an ordained elder in the South Indiana Conference of the United Methodist Church. She has served both urban and town & country churches in that conference. She has one son, Christopher Brian Easley. Ida enjoys leading workshops with women.

Phyllis Pearson Elmore

"Re-Searching" My Mother's Garden

One generation passeth away; and another generation cometh; but the earth abideth forever. —Ecclesiastes 1:4 (KJV)

In her important essay published in 1983, "In Search of Our Mother's Gardens," Alice Walker pays homage to resilient southern black women who, when confronted with their dislocation from Africa, located beauty amid the tedium of their lives by discovering creative outlets for their own frustrated artistry. These women were the quilters, cooks, beauticians, and tillers of the soil, domestics all, who doggedly engaged in their own form of poetry-making, for personal as well as for communal solace.

My own mother, Julia A. Pearson, was born during the second decade of this century in a tiny community called The Promised Land in Abbeville County, South Carolina. This area was made legend by the heinous lynchings that once flourished there. The eldest of six children, my mother thirsted after knowledge of the sciences, which a college education would bring. Because there was no public high school for blacks in The Promised Land—note the irony of that—her family had to board her with relatives in a distant city so that she could attend high school. When family illness and economic realities cut short her quest, my mother had to reformulate her dream. She began to sow her garden elsewhere, beyond her beloved classroom.

My mother satisfied her interest in science by studying cosmetology. She could recite the name of every bone in the head and hand. One of my most vivid memories is that of my mother's "dressing" hair in our country kitchen and of listening to the self-conscious language of the women who were my mother's clients. I was delighted by the sounds of black speech, that collision of formal English with black vernacular that created new meaning. Those women used the mouth as an instrument of persuasion in ritualistic settings. They thereby preserved the linguistic traditions of the race. The quiet rhythms, the occasional riotous laughter, and the hum of common comprehension among the women whom my mother beautified in her kitchen were as much a part of her creative efforts as were her skilled beautician's hands.

My mother's garden, then, was emblematic of her hairdresser's craft. Hence, when sleep eased her from life to death during Holy Week in 1993, my mother left behind a sisterhood of elderly black women who, for a brief season, found camaraderie, confidence, and outer beauty within the garden of my mother's friendship. With my mother, these women are immortalized in the common memory of my South Carolina village. They form a marvelous womanist portrait of an elegant rustic black sisterhood.

Thought for the Day: The past is *not* (contrary to what Sandburg believed) a bucket of ashes.

Phyllis Pearson Elmore holds a degree in rhetoric from Texas Woman's University. She writes and publishes in black women's studies. She teaches rhetoric and literature at North Lake College in Irving, Texas.

Sydne' Charisse Evans

Training a Child for Life

> *Train up children in the way they should go: when they are old, they will not depart from it. —Proverbs 22:6 (NKJV)*

I turned forty-nine years old this year. I take this time to look back and see "how I got over"! I know I haven't done it on my own but with the grace and mercy that God gave my loving parents. Day by day, they were trying to keep my family's heads at or above water level.

There were six girls and four boys to see after. You never know when God, in infinite wisdom, will choose you to be the designated driver! Being the second eldest, when my older sister married early, I had to take on the task of instructor, tutor, laundress, baby-sitter, mediator, minister, surrogate parent, and friend to all of my siblings. As I traveled on my journey, little did I know that every one of those detailed and descriptive roles would round me out to be the woman I am today.

Sitting at the kitchen table, demonstrating math values, correcting homework papers, and braiding hair gave me a well-balanced platform from which I carry out my ministry. Every one of us has a story to tell, so we pass it on with the hope that someone else will be healed or encouraged to live again.

Yes, my road was tedious, and sometimes I had to travel fast! Yet, every day taught me more about the Love we call God. My parents took me through my paces, step by step, so I could pass life's lessons on to others today. My father taught me how to say the Lord's Prayer, how to love Jesus, to praise God, and to honor my parents. Mama taught me how to be a wonderful cook, an outgoing speaker, an excellent listener, and an avid reader. She spent hours on end listening to and watching my siblings and I perform and telling us—as only a mother can do— how gifted we were. My Mama was the one who encouraged my ministry of song. Whenever folks came to our house, be they the insurance agent, plumber, or mail carrier, no matter what I was doing, she insisted that I sing.

The "hope that springs eternal" is the glue that continues to hold our family together during the good times and the bad. Sometimes we get caught up in our individual routines with issues and challenges. But, I make a point of keeping in touch with those who brought me, taught me, and kept me in the precious name of our Lord and Savior, Jesus Christ. Today I can sing because they taught me the value of my songs!

Thought for the Day: Render unto others awesome respect, measure for measure, for the guidance given to you.

Sydne' Charisse Evans is a native Chicagoan and minister of music for The Church of The Open Door. She travels around the nation as a psalmist for churches, conventions, and conferences. A member of Trinity United Church of Christ, she sings because she is happy and free!

Angela Flowers

A Psalm of Gratitude

Sing to the Lord a new song!
—Psalm 96:1 (NIV)

O, I lift up my voice
and sing praise unto the Lord.
I'll shout from the roof top,
from the highest mountain and the lowest
    valley.

For God's steadfast love, mercy, and grace
have kept me, even before I was yet conceived.

Though violence surrounded me as a child
and I was filled with disobedience,
God built a hedge around me and protected me,
so that I could not be destroyed.

Though I turned away
and chose a path of destruction,
God still released angels to encamp all around
    me,
so that death could not overtake me.

Though I walked in a path of wickedness,
worshiping idols of the earth,
God's patience never wavered. God's mercy
    endured.
And God heard my cry, heeded my pleas,
and did not go deaf on me!

God delivered me! God reached down
and brought me out of a horrible pit.
God brought "me" out!
So, I will sing praise unto the Lord
who saved a sinner like me.

God placed me in a church
whose mission is saving souls.
By God's amazing grace I was led
into the marvelous light of salvation.

God's steadfast love
for this child kept me safe.
Now, I am able, by God's grace,

to do unto others as God has done for me.
I show others God's love,
bring them joy,
seek to protect, guide, discipline, and forgive.

God's love, grace, and mercy endure
forever and ever and ever.
I will give thanks
and shout praise unto the Lord.
God is worthy!

Thought for the Day: Thank you, God!

Angela Flowers is a mother and an active "Saving Station" participant with the Hoover United Methodist Church in Little Rock, Arkansas. A liturgical dancer and poet, Angela is employed by the Black Community Developers Program.

Jacqueline P. Ford

With Blinded Eyes, [Grand]Momma Molded Me into a Woman

Therefore, since we are surrounded by such a great cloud of witnesses, let us throw off everything that hinders and the sin that so easily entangles, and let us run with perseverance the race marked out for us. —Hebrews 12:1 (NIV)

During the Easter celebration of 1998, I went back home to North Carolina and visited with my family. Because the occasion was a holiday, I knew that we would take flowers to my grandmother's grave. Before she died in 1988, she told us not to forget about her and to bring flowers to her grave sometimes. My family remembered her request, and the tradition of placing flowers at her grave was an honored demonstration of our love. It allowed us to spend a moment at her gravesite in prayer and reflection. And, I knew her spirit felt our presence there!

However, this holiday as I questioned an aunt and cousin about purchasing Easter lilies, they were slow in responding. Easter morning arrived, and still, we had not purchased lilies. Once again I questioned my family. This time their response was unbelievable; no longer was there a grave to visit. The flood waters of Hurricane Hugo, which had destroyed parts of the Carolinas the previous year, had also caused massive flooding and damage to many cemeteries. As a result, many burial plots and even vaults like my Momma's had been ripped from the ground. Some caskets had opened, and the remains of many loved ones had floated around in waters shoulder-high. My beloved grandmother's grave was destroyed by this storm.

The Monday following Easter, I visited the place where we had buried my Momma. A patch of grass replaced the vault and flower stand that had been a marker for her grave. The shock of finding no resemblance of the burial spot we had chosen and no remnants of having buried the one I loved and cherished was overwhelming. I understood then why my family had chosen not to give me this piece of news. I wailed!

Momma was a beautiful, vivacious, independent, self-sufficient, free-spirited, God-loving woman who had a love for beautiful things. Momma was also blind and had been since a very small child. Yet, despite her inability to see the world through the eyes that most of us take for granted, Momma had a self-confidence bordering on arrogance that made it impossible for blindness to become an obstacle to her. Instead Momma used her lack of sight to show her children and grandchildren that what society deemed a disability did not have to be a hindrance. She set the example for my life.

Momma raised nine children alone after the death of my grandfather. In addition, she raised me and two other granddaughters, as well as providing nurture to my twenty-plus other cousins! Watching Momma "handle" her business—sewing, washing, ironing, cooking, and staying strong under the pressure of family craziness—taught me how to survive. Although

I live in a crazy world calling for young women to prostitute themselves out of need for acceptance and love, I refuse to accept that role in life. Watching Momma kneel down nightly beside her bed taught me by example that there is a God who reigns high and looks low. All I need do is pray.

Momma's unrelenting caring and giving, her generous heart and open arms, taught me how to love generously, to respect others, and most importantly to give of myself unconditionally. Momma left me a solid legacy! Sometimes I have to remind myself that although her physical presence is no longer here, neither in life nor even in death, her spiritual presence is still watching over me, reminding me of the lessons that I failed to learn, and challenging me to apply those teachings. She continues to be a source of guidance, strength, and direction as I try to live up to and be the woman that she modeled before me.

I know that my Momma was guided by God who had given her both the responsibility of her many roles and strength to carry them out. I am persuaded that a loving God knew my Momma could withstand the challenge. So, with her example before me, the challenges and responsibilities that I have been given will not take me down nor make me bow—because anybody who knew her will tell you, *I am "Ms. Reba's child"*!

Thought for the Day: Honor, respect, and cherish the foundation that was laid for you. The very soil of our fore-parents' lives was molded out of love, struggle, and tears. And their legacy was crafted with the strong hands of God.

Jacqueline P. Ford earned her B.A. in human resource training and development at DePaul University in Chicago, and she is employed in the Law School. She strives daily to reach, support, and encourage other young women by setting an example. She is a member of the United Methodist Church in the Chicagoland area.

Beverly Jackson Garvin

In Relationship

> *For surely I know the plans I have for you," says the Lord, "plans for your welfare and not for harm, to give you a future with hope. —Jeremiah 29:11 (NRSV)*

A new ministry to women and girls was born in Detroit, Michigan. This new ministry deals with mother-daughter interactions (mature and young, biological, friends, mentor) and focuses on reconnecting each of us to the Lifeline or Life Source, Jesus the Christ. Lifelines Ministries Incorporated International affirms and embraces relationships in social interaction, encouraging women towards acceptance, love, re-committal, forgiveness—both giving and receiving—as we continue to struggle with our identities as mothers and daughters. This ministry has been born of my own personal labor. I continue to wrestle with being a daughter and primary caregiver to an aging mother, even as I am still learning to be a mother to my own adult daughter who is already out on her own.

Relationships are the key to life. I am charged to teach young girls and their primary female caregivers what they need to know about their personal need for a connection to Jesus Christ, their lifeline. I have the responsibility to point them toward a future that lies before them and an education that can pay off. God has planted in my spirit what has become a lifeline for me. Jeremiah 29:11 is both a declaration and a precious promise: "For surely I know the plans I have for you, says the Lord, plans for your welfare and not for harm, to give you a future with hope."

I had to learn firsthand that, in order for mothers to succeed in raising daughters who are prepared for the twenty-first century, we must ourselves return to Jesus Christ. When our personal relationship with him is established, then we will have the ability to put a prayer hedge of protection around our daughters. Young girls entering puberty are like flowers. Their fragrance permeates the supernatural, and they manifest a beauty that is incomparable. In a repeat of Eve's temptation in the Garden of Eden, this beauty and fragrance that young girls possess causes the enemy to ready another vicious attack in an attempt to snuff out lives with drugs, early pregnancies, destructive habits, ignorance, and low self-esteem. Since each of these tricks were played on me in my youth, my call now is to prevent those attacks from wreaking havoc with other lives.

The enemy will use anything that will stunt maturing growth, potential development, and use of our God-given intelligence. I teach moms that being in relationship with our daughters demands that we know who comes and goes in our households. Being in relationship with our daughters demands that we have good communication skills and that we spend quality time together daily. Telling our daughters that we love them is not enough. (Consider the Book of Ruth for a good biblical role model of mother-daughter relationship.) Being in relationship with our daughters demands care and concern for their well-being, today and in the future. We are mandated to leave no stones unturned until the futures of our girls are sealed and secure.

Girls are God's gifts of pure gold to us. Females have not changed from the beginning. Like Eve, God's daughters still need to be cherished, loved, nurtured, and taught well. I teach today all that I wish my mom had been able to teach me and all that I wish I had been able to teach my daughter! For I have discovered that being in relationship demands that we teach our girls early to love and fear God in reverential awe. We teach them, protect them, and provide daily role models for them by sitting with them in church and studying with them at home, as together we learn the teachings and life of Jesus Christ—Lifelines' mentor for modeling Christianity.

Thought for the Day: Those who find their life will lose it, and those who lose their life for Jesus' sake will find it.

Beverly Jackson Garvin is an ordained elder in the African Methodist Episcopal Church and a graduate of Garrett Evangelical Theological Seminary. She is the founder and executive director of Lifelines Ministries Incorporated International, dedicated to ministry in the life and struggles of females, mature and young. Residing in Detroit, Michigan, she is the proud mother of one daughter, Michele Denise Garvin.

Portia George

Intercepted by Intuition

Always give yourselves fully to the work of the Lord, because you know that your labor in the Lord is not in vain. —*1 Corinthians 15:58 (NIV)*

In 1 Samuel 25, Samuel has just died, and David and his men have fled to the wilderness. While there, they protected the property of Nabal, the husband of Abigail. Scripture tells us that when David heard that Nabal was shearing his sheep, David sent ten of his men to Nabal, reminding him of the protection he and his men had provided and requesting a share in Nabal's feast.

"Not so," said Nabal. In effect, he tells David's men, "Get off my property as you came." When the men returned to David and told him how Nabal had answered, David became angry. "Men, gird on your swords," he ordered, and accompanied by four hundred men, David moved to attack Nabal.

Meanwhile one of Nabal's men went to Abigail, and told her how David had sent messengers to her husband and how Nabal had insulted them. "There's going to be trouble for our master and his household," the servant warned.

Abigail did an about-face in her spirit and intuitively made haste to make amends for her husband's foolishness. She took bread, wine, meat, and other gifts, loaded them on donkeys, and began the interception. As she rode her donkey down the trail, David was moving aggressively up the hill. He was very angry.

When Abigail saw David, the interception was in full swing. She quickly dismounted from her donkey and fell on her face, bowing down on the ground in submission, saying, "I accept all the blame." From her posture of abject humility, she dared to remind David that the battle is the Lord's. "Since God has kept you from taking vengeance into your own hand, let the Lord take care of your enemies," she suggested and offered him the gifts she had brought for him and his men. Relying on her intuition, Abigail reminded David of whose child he was and who was the true Captain of the battlefield.

When David realized in that moment that Abigail had kept him from taking vengeance in his own hands, he blessed Abigail for her good sense—better known as *women's intuition* or the *sixth sense of God*. David accepted Abigail's gifts and went back to his camp in peace.

When Abigail returned home, she found her husband drunk and was unable to *communicate*. In the morning, when she told him the whole story, his heart became as stone, and ten days later he died.

When David heard that Nabal was dead, he rejoiced in the judgment of God, for Nabal had received full punishment for his sins. David wasted no time in asking Abigail to continue to bless his life as his wife.

Abigail teaches us that as women, we have been given a sensitivity to the Spirit, an intuition that has the power to circumvent hasty tempers and influence volatile situations. Sisters, get in tune with that voice inside of you that we call *women's intuition*!

Thought for the Day: God will take care of Christ's own. The Lord has a

way of working things out, in God's own time. Our job is to be intuitively connected and available to the Spirit.

Portia George is the sole proprietor of PG Enterprises, author of three African American Christian children's books, and developer of other products. She is also the founder of Kingdom Kids, a program designed to help children in their journey to know Christ.

Bernadette Glover-Williams

From Loving to Liking Your Family

Put aside your own desires so that you will become patient and godly, gladly letting the Lord have God's way with you. This will make possible the next step, which is for you to enjoy other people and to like them, and finally you will grow to love them deeply. —2 Peter 1:6–7 (TLB)

Since love is the highest virtue, "liking" isn't essential when love is present, right? After all, if you could pick your family members, how many of those you "love" would be retained? Charity may begin at home, but "liking" your family is often the very last virtue to come under a shared roof.

Remember the story about sisters Martha and Mary? Their relationship was characterized by **competition**. The most despised question for any young girl must be: "Why can't you be like your sister?" Is it possible to like a person whose very existence is a mirror reflecting your insufficiency and is imposed as a model, demanding that you become her clone in order to be accepted? In family systems where support and love are rationed like government cheese during a depression, it is hard to "like" a rival with whom you compete for attention, affirmation, and understanding.

Remember the story about Joseph and his brothers? Theirs was a family of **typecast** characters. Families share the same cast of characters as those in other human groups. Champions, challengers, catalysts, assenters, complainers, saints, sinners, seers, comforters, scapegoats, and counselors all have a part in the kin script. However, when "deviants" stray from their prescribed roles, their creativity often causes the rest of the cast to become disparaging critics. Don't you struggle to "like" people who insist that you live out some old, unresolved intergenerational issues and dreams as if those issues and dreams were your own?

Remember the story of the prodigal son and his older brother? They attempted to deny their relationship and the **permanence** of their kinship ties. Our families aren't often impressed with our lofty campaigns that tout us above them and our "roots"! They know us. Our private Pandora's boxes are public domain to them, and we're uneasy with relationships we can't divorce. How awkward it is trying to "like" people who will always be in my life, remembering me "when"! My shame and arrogance would prefer to love them from afar rather than "like" them up close.

Yet, I have discovered some strategies that can help us transition from loving to "liking" our families. First, punch holes in your negative associations with family members by seeing them as human beings, not siblings; forgive them and release them from the dungeon of your disappointment. Then, ask yourself, why is my sister, my sister? If we have the families that we do by sovereign omniscient choice, and if Proverbs is right that "iron sharpens iron," then my family is a corporate partner in my development and destiny. By divine design, something in them is *for me* and something in me is *for them*, mutually inextricable in purpose.

Finally, allow yourself to encounter your family as if for the first time, and permit the burst of interpersonal chemistry normally indicative of a "getting to know you" situation. You might actually find that your family is likable after all!

Thought for the Day: Treat your family as strangers! Practice hospitality!

Bernadette Glover-Williams is married to Edward W. Williams. She holds a D.Min. degree and is part of the pastoral staff at The Cathedral — Second Baptist Church in Perth Amboy, New Jersey.

Stephany D. Graham

Faith Power

> *Count it all joy, my sisters, when you
> meet various trials, for you know that
> the testing of your faith produces stead-
> fastness. —James 1:2–3 (RSV)*

I was always looked upon as the strong one
in my family. I found that label to be burdensome and shortsighted on my mother's part. I
got tired of everyone coming to me with their
problems and sad stories. I was only a child. I
don't remember demonstrating any unusual
ability to cope or to maintain my composure
during difficult times. In fact, I was always the
one to overreact and then find a quiet place to
weep and pray. I knew that I was absolutely
powerless over the hard life that had been dealt
to me and my family. I knew that if we were to

overcome, we would have to rely on a strength greater than any of us.

I realized early on that I needed God to walk with me through the mean streets of my life. I now know that only by God's grace was I one of the few who survived those streets with minimal scarring. Now that I am an adult, I realize that, in identifying me as "the strong one," Mama was acknowledging the gift of faith God had placed within me. She saw something in me then that I still have difficulty recognizing in myself.

This gift of faith has made it possible for me to stay married even when all of the odds were against us. It has made it possible for me to remain determined even when the church decided that they were not ready to call a woman preacher. It has guided me as I have journeyed through racist religious institutions. It has guided me when I've returned home to find the street war escalating. It guided me when I lost the baby that I thought I could not conceive. It guides me when I am faced with the seduction of power, privilege, and prestige. It guides me, when all of this becomes too much, to that quiet place to weep and pray.

In that quiet place I am reminded of my role in my family, in my ministry, and in my relationship with God. I am reminded that the battle is not mine, that it belongs to the Lord. For whatever reason, the Lord has chosen to use me as a vessel to accomplish a part of God's agenda. Mine is not an uncommon story. It is a story shared by African American women throughout our history. My grandmother was one of those who endured and overcame obstacles that might have pushed my faith beyond its limits. Many women too numerous to name have demonstrated unprecedented courage, raw determination, and unswerving faith.

Today, African American women, the mothers of civilization, are being destroyed at catastrophic rates by drugs, incarceration, HIV, and hatred. The time is long overdue for those of us who have had a faith strong enough to survive our periods of captivity to return to help our sisters recognize their source of strength. We must be mother, sister, daughter to them and envision with them the gift of faith. As African American women, we must weep and then assume our role as the strong ones in the family!

Thought for the Day: My weakest place gives God space!

Stephany D. Graham currently serves as the Associate for African American Leadership Training and Resource Development for the Presbyterian Church (U.S.A.). She received her M.Div. degree from the Princeton Theological Seminary in 1993 and is currently working toward her D.Min. at the Samuel D. Proctor School of Theology at the Virginia Union University.

Faye S. Gunn

Strength to Endure

> *My grace is sufficient for you, for my strength is made perfect in weakness.*
> *—2 Corinthians 12:9 (NKJV)*

My calling into the ministry has not been without trials and tears, heartaches and headaches. But I count it all joy and give thanks to God for strength to endure. Every now and then I reflect upon my experiences which have strengthened my faith journey.

One experience was my academic preparation for the ministry. Women who have families and who are called into ministry have an awesome responsibility. Firmly believing in the word of God that tells us to "study to show thyself approved unto God," I enrolled in the nontraditional hours program at Virginia Union University School of Theology. To this day, I know I made the right decision. For three and a half years, I commuted each week approximately 240 miles from suburban Washington, D.C., to Richmond, Virginia, for classes. But the sudden change in schedule that required my being away from home on Friday evenings and Saturday mornings was especially difficult for our son Rodney, an active teenage honor student.

From Rodney's facial expressions alone, I easily detected his feeling of despondency in response to what seemed like rejection by his mother. He had long been active in sports and at church, and I had attended nearly all of his games. But now, if his father had to work late, he was left to ride with other parents to his games and other activities. At age fourteen, this was a difficult time for him.

We read in Proverbs, "Train up children in the way they should go and when they get old they will not depart from it." Rodney grew up in the church and Sunday school. At age seven, he gave his life to Christ. We are blessed parents because Rodney never gave us any trouble that required our having to go to his school or to court, despite my being away from home many weekends. I believe he was able to endure peer pressure and the trauma of that critical time in his life because of his love for Jesus and our weekly family devotions and discussions. Perhaps what was most important was our constantly telling him that Jesus loved him and so did we. If our children are to have the strength to endure, they must know Jesus for themselves.

There were times when my schedule was just as hard for me as it was for Rodney. As I would drive down I-95, tears would fill my eyes. In those tearful moments, I wanted to give up, turn around, and go back home. Like the apostle Paul, we, too, have our thorns in the flesh. I take no credit for having had the stamina to endure. Praise be to God! God's strength and grace are sufficient to bring us through in our times of weakness. In the words of the psalmist, "Weeping may endure for a night, but joy cometh in the morning." The morning has come by the strength of the indwelling Spirit, who taught me to hold on and to hold out. Being prepared academically has brought not only fulfillment to my ministry but joy to my entire family. We have Jesus' joy as we continue to serve and worship the Lord together!

Thought for the Day: Let us not grow weary while doing good, for in due season we shall reap if we do not faint. (Galatians 6:9 NKJV)

Faye S. Gunn is the assistant minister at the historic Alfred Street Baptist Church in Alexandria, Virginia. She holds an M.Div. from the School of Theology, Virginia Union University and a D.Min. from Wesley Theological Seminary. She serves on the board of trustees for the Nannie Hellen Burroughs School in Washington, D.C.

Deborah Jean Hampton

My Life Is in God's Hand

Keep me safe, O God, for in you I take refuge. —Psalm 16:1 (NIV)

The Lord has been really good to me. I have learned to listen, look for, and feel the blessings as they come, and they have come in a varied number of ways. As I spoke about the importance of quality church-related childcare programs in front of fifty distinguished pastors of a local conference of pastors, the pastors seemed bored with the subject matter. Many were making other conversation. Just as I thought that I was "sinking to rise no more," one of the influential pastors began to show interest and asked thought-provoking questions. The questions stimulated other pastors. The pastors began to dialogue about the calling of churches to create quality programs that support children in families.

There was an angel in the midst of the storm, an angel who continues to help and assist me as I work on behalf of all of God's children. That angel undergirds the work that I do and directs my path. My confidence in that angel makes me think of the song I love sing to myself: "No matter what will come my way, my life is in God's hand." God sends anointing spirits to carry me through each situation in which I find myself (Hebrews 1:14). I have learned to depend on those angels and attune my spirit to search for them when I am in need.

The Lord has directed my path in times of trouble and dismay. God will make a way out of nowhere to lift me up and carry me through. God is the author and designer of my work, the silent presence in every time of distress. "O how I love Jesus," the Alpha and Omega of my being. Thanks be to my Lord for always being there as my protector and my guide.

Thought for the Day: You don't have to worry or be afraid. Jesus Christ protects all who serve in his name.

Deborah Jean Hampton is presently the executive director of the Ecumenical Child Care Network. She has a masters degree from Erikson Institute and has done further study at Erikson in the field of special needs, serving as a mentor and instructor at Erikson Institute's Bridge to Professional Leadership. Her professional affiliations include being board chairperson of the Chicago Metropolitan Association for the Education of Young Children.

Hattie G. Harris

Making a Difference

Encourage the young people to be self-controlled. In everything set them an example by doing what is good. In your teaching show integrity, seriousness, and soundness of speech. . . . —Titus 2:6–8 (NIV)

A litany of descriptive words is being used to describe today's African American youth. Three that caught my attention are "belligerent," "disrespectful," and "indifferent." Listening to these negative labels causes some people to conclude that a large number of youth will face a future filled with a plethora of insurmountable odds. Without a doubt, this is a valid conclusion, but a difference can be made. Instead of promoting a sense of helplessness or hopelessness, I view this crisis as a golden opportunity for putting faith in action. African American women in African American churches are developing action plans to make a difference in the lives of our at-risk youth.

Now, the question may be asked: Why African American women and African American churches? I submit two reasons. First, the home has traditionally been a molding place for shaping character and developing productive family members. From an historical perspective, the African American woman has always been the cohesive backbone that kept the family together. This fact confirms that we have the ability and the tenacity to make a difference in the lives of our youth.

Secondly, as a spiritual reservoir, the church has also complemented the home in developing spiritual and moral values. In light of this, what accounts for the moral breakdown in our families? Chief among a number of reasons is generational amnesia, for it is obvious that some mothers "forgot" to transmit a legacy of values! Admittedly, times are different, but the need for values is just as great today as it was when we were children.

One of the first steps toward nurturing value-conscious youth is for African American women to pray individually and collectively for insight, wisdom, understanding, and direction. Next, we need to structure a daily devotional timetable in our homes. Doing this will enable children and youth to see that God should have a prominent place in daily life. Daily devotions will also be an opportunity for them to develop understanding of biblical texts and skills in reading Scripture and praying aloud, skills that will eventually develop their faith in God. Additionally, African American women must show youth outside the home that we have confidence in them. As a retired educator, I have seen a number of youth excel simply because I had faith in them.

In making a difference for our youth, we need to use every tangible means possible to show them that we care. This is a prerequisite for generating a positive sense of self-respect. For how can we expect our youth to respect others, authority, and human life if they have low self-esteem? Therefore, we must exert every effort toward providing them with encouragement, love, discipline, support, wholesome activities, quality time, and listening ears.

Since women comprise a large percentage of church memberships, a focused vision on making a difference for youth in African American churches can underscore the strength inherent in unity. A unified group of women working on behalf of our youth can have an awesome impact. I strongly feel that, if the church is to fulfill the mission that Jesus mandated, we must minister to the needs of people from an holistic perspective through ministries such as parenting workshops, rites of passage, tutoring, language, math, science, and computer enrichment, Bible competitions, sports, sexuality appreciation, and education about healthy lifestyles.

Finally, if we are genuinely concerned about making a difference in the lives of our youth, we will accept the challenge to love them, to nurture them, and to role model for them the lasting values that we each so desperately need in our lives. They must be led to believe that "I can do all things through Christ who strengthens me."

Thought for the Day: With God's help, we can make a difference!

Hattie G. Harris, a retired educator, is director of Christian education at the Cedar Grove Baptist Church, in Simpsonville, South Carolina. She is also a faculty member in the Progressive National Baptist Congress and the National Baptist Congress, USA, Inc. Presently, she is pursuing an M.A. in Christian education from Erskine Theological Seminary in Due West, South Carolina.

Linda H. Hollies

Spiritual Gifts

Your gift makes room for you. . . .
—Proverbs 18:16 (KJV, paraphrased)

They rejected me again! A group with whom I've worked long and diligently had need for leadership. My name was nominated. As I looked around the gathering and recognized sisters I've worked with through the years, I began to count my votes. I began to formulate my acceptance speech. I saw myself, out front, leading this sisterhood forward. But, when the votes were tallied, I was not the winner. They had rejected me again!

It hurt. I didn't feel good about their rejection of my gifts. I was angry. Is this how sisters repay deeds of kindness? I left the session and went to the treadmill to walk off the stress, to step on their faces, and to permit God to restore my inner tranquility. As I walked, not going anywhere, I remembered. As I walked, not moving in distance from their presence, I recalled. And, as I walked, stepping quickly in the very same spot, I reflected upon the spiritual gifts I had offered to my sisters.

God has gifted me with great faith. I will step out with no money, little visible support, and have tremendous vision to bring the will of God to fruition. I didn't ask for this gift. I didn't have sense enough to request it! But, my gift of faith has helped me pull mighty mountains down! This gift from God has made room for me in places and with persons, at times and in situations where I clearly understood, "This is the Lord's doing, and it's marvelous in my eyes."

God has gifted me with the ability to teach and to preach. As a child with Pentecostal roots, there was little I was permitted to do for entertainment. Almost everything, especially "frivolous" athletic playing, was labeled sin. Books became my friends. The public library became my playground. My world was widened by information stored on written pages. I soaked up knowledge. The hunger within me grew. I became a resource of opinions beyond my limited world. People listened when I spoke. People learned from a young girl. I was sought after, referred to, and sent for time and time again. I boldly proclaimed the revealed wisdom I had gathered. "God has given me the tongue of the learned, that I should know how to speak a word in season to those who are weary," proclaimed the prophet Isaiah (Isaiah 50:4 KJV). Like him, my gift is from God, who ordered my steps as a child to have a love affair with words and the Living Word. This gift has certainly made room for me.

God has gifted me with the gift of administration. Of course I've taken management courses. Indeed I've read the collective theories of effectively managing people and resources. But, God has been the one to open the doors for me to work in three of the top ten American industries as a manager. In these places I have learned how to sift through the theories for what works for and through me. And, I've learned how to discard all those methods that effectively disregard people! I've learned how to see the "big" picture and then to plot the steps that will take us there! Today, as a church consultant, I am served well by this gift. It has helped many others to be more effective in their ministries.

As I walked the treadmill that day, I remembered that all of my gifts come from God. And, I recalled that God has *always* had my very best interest and development in mind. When the walk was over, so was my short pity-party. Clearly, that position was not the place where God needed me at that particular time. Many other opportunities have already been divinely designed just for me. My gifts and giftedness will take me there!

Perhaps you have known the experience of rejection, too! The good news is that God has not rejected you! Thanks be unto the Gifting God!

Thought for the Day: Know your gifts. Your gift will make room for you!

Linda H. Hollies is the director of Outreach Ministries for the West Michigan Annual Conference of the United Methodist Church. She is founder and executive director of **Woman to Woman Ministries, Inc.,** an educational resource agency for Women of Color, and is the author of seven books. She is the loving mother of three children, a grandmother, and is always looking for creative methods of being God's trumpet in Zion!

Grian Eunyke Hollies-Anthony

Standing Still in the Midst of a Mess

> ***Therefore, my beloved, be steadfast,
> immovable, always abounding in the
> work of the Lord, knowing that your
> labor is not in vain!*** *—1 Corinthians
> 15:58 (NKJV)*

I am a young woman, only twenty-eight years
old, but some days it seems like I've lived for
ages! Like many of you, I'm going through
some things! My life often seems long because
of the choices I've made.

I'm a recovering addict working a 12-step
program. This is a daily practice of principles
and a spiritual connection with a Higher Power,
whom I choose to call God. If you don't know
someone with an addiction, I'm sure television

has given you an idea of the lifestyle. I can truly say that I have lived two lives in one lifetime. I have been to hell, stayed, played, suffered, and cried out for help. Because God is good, I was picked up, dusted off, and sent to tell others of this new freedom and happiness.

Considering the things I've been through, life should be just lovely—right? Wrong! Life continues to be life. I have a new baby girl. But, I am separated from my husband. My knight in shining armor turned out to be a human being with flaws and shortcomings like me. I have the opportunity to work in the recovery field with others like me—but surprise! I have problems on the job too.

If we add this all up, I'm a tired, stressed-out, lonely, and frustrated single mom. When I see the commercial welcoming me to the warm waters of Jamaica, I want to run! Run from problems, bills, bad relationships, and all the drama of life. The beautiful people lounging on the beach couldn't have my problems. Or could they?

When life feels heavy on my shoulders, I have to sit back, be still, reflect, and pray. I must remember my "sheros": Grandmother, Doretha, Aunt Eunice, Granny Lucinda, and Mom. I know life threw them for a loop too. But they were strong African American women who stood firmly planted when the storms of life hit! They sang songs, cried out to the Lord, and went on with their heads held high. These women taught me that I had a friend who would bear my burdens, fight my battles, and be that shoulder to cry on if I would only ask and allow.

That all sounds good, but Angela Basset looked like she had the right idea in *Waiting to Exhale* when she vented her anger by burning her unfaithful husband's clothes! Would it hurt if I just cursed him out real good to let him know who I am? The hardest thing to do is nothing!

Today I am a child of God. I know God will fight my battles and make my enemies my footstool! My weapon for life's battles is prayer. As long as I do what God requires of me, I no longer have to fight. God's got my back! All I have to do is stand still and know God.

Life still goes on, and I have more storms ahead of me. I have an inner peace knowing that everything is going to be all right as long as I work my program, for life holds a promise for the "good of those who serve the Lord." Eugene Peterson, author of *The Message*, put it best. "With all this going for us, my dear, dear friends,

Book title: _____

Your comments: _____

Where did you hear about this book: _____

Reasons why you bought this book: (check all that apply) □ Subject □ Author □ Attractive Cover

□ Recomendation of a friend □ Recomendation of a Reviewer □ Gift □ Other _____

If purchased: Bookseller _____ City _____ State _____

Please send me a Judson Press catalog. I am particularly interested in: (check all that apply)

1. □ African American
2. □ Baptist History/Beliefs
3. □ Bible Study
4. □ Children's Books
5. □ Christian Education
6. □ Christian Living
7. □ Church Leadership
8. □ Church Supplies
9. □ Devotional/Prayer
10. □ Preaching/Sermon Helps
11. □ Self-Help
12. □ Women's Issues

Yes, add my name to your mailing list!

Name (print) _____ Phone _____

Street _____

City _____ State _____ Zip _____

Please send a Judson Press catalog to my friend:

Name (print) _____ Phone _____

Street _____

City _____ State _____ Zip _____

Judson Press • P.O. Box 851 • Valley Forge, PA 19482-0851 • 1-800-458-3766 • FAX (610) 768-2107 stand your ground. And don't hold back. Throw yourselves into the work of Jesus Christ, confident that nothing you do for him is a waste of time or effort."

Thought for the Day: When life's storms are raging, stand still, hold God's hand, and know that you have the victory! Hallelujah!

Grian Eunyke Hollies-Anthony is the beloved daughter of Charles H. Hollies and Linda H. Hollies. She is parent of three children, Giraurd, Gamel, and Symphony. She is an active participant in the "Life Saving Station" of Hoover United Methodist Church in Little Rock, Arkansas.

Janet Hopkins

Hugs I Never Got

Let us love, not in word or speech, but in truth and action. —1 John 3:18 (NRSV)

Hugs are very important in our lives for they tell us that we are loved and cared about. Hugs provide warmth just as a blanket does on a cold wintery night. When I was a little girl, my parents never hugged or kissed me. I am sure they loved me in their own special way. If only they had known how much I longed for just a hug. That hug would have spoken to my heart. I really would have felt so special and affirmed in my little world.

I found myself struggling as a young mother, not being able to hug my children. When I realized that I was denying my children the very hugs that I so wanted to receive, I knew that I would have to change. I consciously worked at making sure every day that I hugged and kissed my children. In the beginning it was difficult, but in time it became easier until, finally, hugging became a part of who I was. I wanted to change my behavior and that was only the beginning of the many changes that took place in my life.

My children are all grown up now, and I still hug and kiss them whenever I am with them. I sometimes wonder if the inability to hug and kiss is hereditary, however, because my youngest daughter does not like me or her siblings to hug her! Of course, I sneak in a hug anyway, and she laughs and tells me to get away.

As a pastor I get lots of hugs from the members—and I love it. I have also found other ways to hug myself. I surround myself with people who are beautiful on the inside and with beautiful things. Every room in my home hugs me with wonderful black art, delicate trinkets, pictures of friends and family, lively colors, beautiful dishes, and 24-karat gold silverware. And of course my bedroom is warm and bright with luscious bedding that hugs me at night as I slumber and sleep. As well, I have a personal flair for clothes that hug my body every day—

wonderful silks, soft satins, lush cottons, and any other fabric that feels good surrounding me.

I will never ever be without hugs again! I have found a way to surround my life in hugs, as you can plainly see. The most special hugs of all are those I receive from the God who "walks with me and talks with me and tells me I'm God's own." The Great Lover is ever present in my life. Omnipresent love is wrapped around me day and night. Hugs do not have to be missing in our lives. There are many ways to give ourselves a hug. Why not hug yourself right now?

Thought for the Day: A hug a day will keep you smiling all day.

Janet Hopkins is a native of Chicago. She received her doctorate from McCormick Theological Seminary in Chicago and is an ordained elder in the United Methodist Church. Janet pastors Mandell and Olivet U.M.C. on the Westside of Chicago. She is an excellent hugger!

Darlene Moore James

Quiet Time with God

Then cometh Jesus with them unto a place called Gethsemane, and saith unto the disciples, Sit ye here, while I go and pray yonder. —Matthew 26:36 (KJV)

Taking time to be quiet with God? That's hard to imagine. Quiet time with God is like a deferred dream—impossible to believe that we as Christian working women can actually get to a place where we model Jesus' example. Jesus even managed to spend quiet time with God *and* quality time with those who were significant to him! Yes, Jesus practiced the discipline of quiet, individual meditation. He went away, set himself apart, and prayed. That time alone with God was his strength. It enabled, encouraged, and equipped him to handle all God had called him to do.

In today's busy and fast-paced society, it is eye-opening to view how we Christians spend our time. We say many times how we love God and family, yet we spend very little quiet time with either of them.

All too often when we get up in the morning, we are busy fixing breakfast, combing hair, packing lunches, answering phone calls, and making long "to do" lists of the twenty-five things we have to do today. Then, of course, we are still making mental notes to pick the children up, go to the store, drop Joshua or Jasmine off at karate class, prepare dinner, go to the church, pay bills, go to open house at school, return phone calls, make small talk with the family, wash a load of clothes, pack for our out-of-town job-related trip, pick up the teenager from work, iron, pray, put the children to bed, and fall in bed ourselves.

Then we pray that by the grace of God we will get up the next morning and repeat this endless and time-consuming cycle of business, again. The balance of how we all too often spend our time is off. We all should periodically do a time-check on when we last saw a sunrise, a sunset, walked in the park, sat on our porch, picked four-leaf clovers, sat down and listened to nature's music.

I received a revelation about quiet time and quality time with God about a month after receiving my first pastoral appointment in June of 1991. I was the first female, full-time, appointed pastor of a three-point charge in the Louisiana Annual Conference. I preached three different times in three different towns every Sunday. Yes, I was busy and about God's business—so I thought. I was keeping eighty-five to ninety-five hour work weeks! I believed I was doing what I loved and what I was called by God to do. But my life and God's ministry had no depth or balance.

In July 1991, I broke my left ankle in a freak accident. I was told I would never walk without a limp. During my healing time, God revealed how essential in life is quiet time. I thank God for that healing time because it allowed me to have precious time alone with the Lord. I thank God for those quiet times.

Since 1991 I have been intentional about spending quiet time with God. I get up an hour earlier than anyone in the house; I sit quietly at my desk for ten minutes when I arrive at work; I take my days off; I take my vacation; I even take a couple of three-day getaways each year to spend healing away from home—at a hotel, a conference center, or a monastery. Also the week after Easter I go away for a week of consecration (not vacation), away from my pastoral appointment setting, with no phone calls, fax, beepers, cell phones, and I spend time with God, listening for spiritual direction for my life and my God-given ministry. As a result of these times of quiet, alone with God, I am moving straight ahead, walking in miracles every day.

In November of 1995, when I was spending quiet time on a pilgrimage in the Holy Land, God began to reveal in my spirit that something significant was about to happen. Within a week of returning, I received word from the district superintendent that I was being appointed to a living, growing, praying, tithing, and visionary 450-member congregation in Slidell, Louisiana. Hartzell-Mt. Zion UMC had asked for me by name. I was to be the first African American female in the Louisiana Conference to receive such an appointment. Well, today is three years later, and the appointment is doing quite well. Last year we won numerous souls for Christ and raised $91,000.00 over our set budget for a Family Life Center. Somebody please say, "GLORY!"

Oh yeah, I still have a long list of things to do, but at the top of my list is quiet time with God and quality time with the family God has given me.

Thought for the Day: Spend quiet time with God every day; pray, meditate, listen, and that time will only bring blessings your way. Showers of blessings!

Darlene Moore James is a ministerial product of Newell United Methodist Church in Mandeville, Louisiana. She is the author of *Sista Pearl* and *I Am the Preacher's Child.* She pastors Hartzell-Mt. Zion UMC in Slidell, Louisiana. She is the mother of Joshua II.

Jacquelyn Jeunai

I Lost My Baby, but Not My Mind

A Thirty-Year Journey from a Burnt-Out Place to a Spirit-Filled Space

> *The Advocate, the Holy Spirit, whom God will send in my name, will teach you everything, and remind you of all that I have said to you. Peace I leave with you; my peace I give to you. I do not give to you as the world gives. Do not let your hearts be troubled, and do not let them be afraid. —John 14:26–27 (NRSV)*

Hisssss, click. Hisssss, click. Hisssss. Silence. The machine was turned off. The sound of its life-sustaining work ended. Later, as I stood in the hall, my strength drained from my body, and I began to slide slowly down, down into an abyss of swirling, smothering gloom. My baby girl was dead. My first-born baby daughter was dead. At nine years young. She was killed in a fire that took both our first home and our dreams.

Almost thirty years have passed since I buried my daughter. The days and months of madness that followed are now blurred in my mind. However, what stands out with three-dimensional clarity is the Holy Spirit—clothed in full humanity—coming to me. They came—Holy Spirit-filled servants of the Lord, obedient to God's direction, ministering to me.

In my "sanctified imagination," this is how I chronicle my journey from that burned out physical place to an inner space filled with the peace of the Holy Spirit. I hear God speaking to the Holy Spirit, saying, "Go to my child, Jacquelyn. Tell her I love her and am with her, even now."

And one day a friend said to me, "Honey, you know there is a God who loves you. After all you have been through, you're still in your right mind! Hold on girl, the Lord is with you!" I heard her message and I held on.

Later God said to the Holy Spirit, "Teach her to trust in me, to test me and to deepen her faith."

And one evening, a Vacation Bible School teacher sat with me many hours after class. He said to me, "Take little tiny steps of faith. Just try a little test. God is able and equal to the task." I accepted this challenge, and my faith deepened.

"Tell her I loved her and all humanity so much that I sent my Son to die for their sins. Guide her to an understanding of my love, of salvation and eternal life," said God to the Holy Spirit.

I was led to enter a theological seminary certificate program. My focus was on the salvific gift of Jesus Christ. My goal was to study theology in order to become a more knowledgeable lay person.

And then God said to the Holy Spirit, "Tell her I have called her to ordained ministry. Direct her, fill her in order that she might lift me up so that I can draw others through her."

On a speaking tour, I took a side trip to visit a church whose pastor had impressed me with her messages and her humble spirit. During our conversation over lunch, she said, "Have you considered chaplaincy as your ministry?" Surprised, I stopped chewing briefly. What a strange question, I thought. Hadn't I just explained that I didn't feel called to pastoral ministry of a local church? And now here she was, ignoring my statements and suggesting a chaplaincy ministry—which, by the way, I knew nothing about.

Years later, after graduating with a masters degree from theological seminary and completing CPE (Clinical Pastoral Education) residency, I accepted a position as a hospice chaplain.

"Hello, you must be the chaplain," says the woman who has opened the door. I step across the threshold, preparing to minister to this family.

"Yes, I am the hospice chaplain."

I love my work. I minister faithfully. Through the power of the Holy Spirit and the loving nurture of many "saints" of God, I made it through the madness of grief. I did lose my baby. But, thank God, I didn't lose my mind!

Thought for the Day: Jesus promised to send the Holy Spirit to comfort and guide me. Today I will stand on that promise.

Jacquelyn Jeunai, a native of Minneapolis, Minnesota, is an ordained minister and a hospice chaplain for HealthEast. She is a member of Fellowship Missionary Church where she serves on the ministerial team.

Diane Harris Johnson

Brick by Brick (Bill by Bill)

So we built the wall; and all the wall was joined together. . . . For the people had a mind to work. —Nehemiah 4:6 (RSV)

The mail carrier came today. And once again I dreaded going through the mail. Bills, second notice, final notice, cutoff notice. When are they going to *notice* that I don't have the money to pay these bills? Wait a minute. When are "they" going to notice? The real question is when am *I* going to notice and *do* something about this dreadful situation? How do I get out of this economically oppressing and financially depressing mess? The answer is: the same way I got into it—bill by bill.

I am reminded of the story found in the Book of Nehemiah. In the fifth chapter, Nehemiah was faced with an economic crisis among the workers. Apparently some among them were charging high interest on their loans, and to make matters worse, those who owed money were being forced to sell their children into slavery to pay off their old debts.

Today, many of us find ourselves in this same situation. We may not literally sell our children, but we are putting their economic futures on the auction block. Some of us are so far in debt that it seems we will have to sell our children's future to get out of debt. We refinance the house, using the equity to pay off our bills, or we take out a second mortgage, adding new debt on top of old debt, or we borrow from friends, family members, our church, or anyone willing to loan us money, no matter what the cost. We find ourselves paying high interest rates over long periods of time, encumbering our financial freedom, becoming victims of economic bondage.

And in the midst of it all, we hope and pray that by the time our children need money to go to college, buy their first car, or just get a jump on life, we will have been out of debt long enough—to qualify for a loan.

No, no, no! We have it all wrong. The only way out of debt is to repay the old debt without creating new debt. Seems impossible, but it is not. With God, all things are possible. How shall we do this? Brick by brick—or rather, bill by bill—we can restore the bottom line.

Having made this resolution for myself, I looked at each of my bills and laid them out on the table, somewhat as a contractor would gather the materials needed to rebuild a broken-down wall. I placed bills (bricks) in one pile, placed all my income in another pile, and in the last pile listed all necessary living expenses. The brick pile was pretty high, but like Nehemiah, I prayed that God would show me favor to do this work. I prayed that God would give me the discipline to stick to my business plan, changing my burdensome economic ways of life forever.

The first thing I did was call each of my creditors, informing them of my over-indebtedness and requesting their assistance in restructuring my current debt. In other words, I implied to them that was in *our* best interest to lower my minimum monthly payment. Then I had to make some hard decisions. I had to *reduce expenses*—reduce expenditures on hair appointments and nail appointments, make do with my present wardrobe, reduce the cable bill, telephone bill, utility bills, and grocery bills, cut out fast food from my diet (and budget), and last but not least, eliminate NSF (non-sufficient funds) check fees.

Next, I sought ways to increase my income. What did I have that I could sell at a yard sale? Why not call a few friends who were also going through a financial crisis? The bigger the yard sale, the more buyers. I used *all* the money from the yard sale and any other extra revenue received to apply to the bill with the lowest balance. I figured that if I paid off the bill with the lowest balance as soon as possible, then I could apply the monies formerly paid to that creditor to the bill with the next lowest balance.

The goal is to always pay on time and pay more than the minimum payment required. Once one bill is paid off, apply both former payments to the next lowest balance. You got it! Soon you will have your bills under control. You will feel good about your economic future and your credit will be restored.

Remember, learn from your mistakes. Learn to say no. Don't buy something unless you can pay for it, now. With my new method of practicing sound stewardship, I did rebuild the walls of my credit. So can you!

Thought for the Day: Dear God, thank you for making a way out of what seems to be no way. Thank you for restoring our fields, vineyards, olive orchards, houses, money, grain, wine, and oil (Nehemiah 5:11). Thank you for restoring my joy. Amen.

Diane Harris Johnson is the founding pastor of Jerusalem African Methodist Episcopal Church in Clinton, Maryland. She earned her M.Ed., M.B.A., and M.Div. degrees from Howard University and her D.Min. degree from United Theological Seminary. She is the board chair for the Christian African American Booksellers Assoc., Inc. (CAABA) and co-owner of Gospel Notes Records and Books.

Erma L. Kyser

A Virtuous Woman

The wise woman builds her house, but the foolish tears it down with her own hands. —Proverbs 14:1 *(NRSV)*

When I count my blessings, I always remember to count my family. We have been so greatly blessed by God that I love telling others about all the Lord has done for us. My mother and father were blessed to have fourteen children, eight boys and six girls. My mother is eighty-six years of good age and is still in reasonably good health. All fourteen of her children have survived. Our family has remained close, even though some of us live in different states. We owe this closeness to our parents, who taught us how to appreciate each other.

Oh! I won't say that we have not had some tumultuous times. Many things have been quite hard to overcome, but because of our love for each other, we know how to forgive and let God heal the pain.

In my work with children, I find that those children who do not have strong family support and ties are often the children who are more difficult to handle. They are missing a vital link in their lives—the benefit of being taught, loved, and supported by strong family ties.

When I read in Proverbs 31:10 that a virtuous woman is worth far more than precious gems, I think about my mother. She is a virtuous woman, and her price is indeed far above rubies. She has been the mainstay in our family. She kept us together. She did the teaching, instilling in us the moral values that have not left us. She built her house like the wise woman described in Proverbs 14:1.

At eighty-six, my mother still receives the highest respect from her children. We know that God has blessed us and kept us together all these years. Sometimes, as I look at our family, I shiver at this blessing. Despite our flaws and failings, God is diligent in molding and creating each of us.

Thankfully, God is not looking for any perfect person. The Creator already knows that we are imperfect. The Lord expects us to be wise, to be virtuous, to honor our Maker and each other, but in reality, God can use an ass to accomplish the Lord's purpose. It would not be the first time God did so (Numbers 22:22–35)!

I am thankful that the Lord provides not only the Holy Spirit but also spirit-filled people, like my mother and virtuous women like her, to train, teach, advise, and guide me. Sisters, let us pray that we will become like these wise women and build our houses on the foundation of God's Word and Spirit.

Thought for the Day: Lord, let me always be aware of your guidance for my life. Give me the patience to wait on you and to know that every step I take and the direction I go is the plan you have laid out for my life. Teach me to build my house with wisdom.

Erma L. Kyser is a high school counselor in Sacramento, California, and publisher of her own religious newsletter, *Exceedingly Joyful.* She has been an educator for twenty-four years and is vice president of the Sacramento City Teachers Association. She received her B.A. from the University of California at Davis, her M.S. in school counseling from the University of La Verne, and doctoral studies curriculum in clinical psychology.

Linda Lee

Doing a Backfloat

Delight yourself in the Lord and God will give you the desires of your heart. Commit your way to the Lord; trust in God and God will do this; God will make your righteousness shine like the dawn, the justice of your cause like the noonday sun. —Psalm 37:4–6 (NIV)

I am not much of a swimmer. In fact, what I do best in large bodies of water is float. Anything else is a struggle—beating the water, gasping for air, choking on all the unwanted water I inhale in the midst of trying not to drown.

All too often, as women of African descent, we find ourselves in the middle of struggle. Sometimes, those struggles are small ones, like whether to fix fish or chicken for dinner. Too often, however, they are larger struggles, like whether we should stay with that man who has fallen short in some way or how we should discipline this child because of unacceptable behavior. Then, there's the ultimate struggle— the one we have with God and therefore, with ourselves.

We struggle with God because we sometimes have an approach-avoidance relationship with God. We approach God with our requests and needs and sometimes our praise and thanks. But when things really get rough, we often avoid God at first, turning away, nursing our wounds, and fighting the biggest battles alone. We beat the water. We gasp for air. We choke on all the unwanted stuff we swallow, trying to keep from drowning. Things could be so much easier on us. The choice is ours: we could just do a back-float in the Holy Spirit. Then our struggle with God would be over.

But no wonder we struggle with God! The God we've been taught to worship looks like the very ones who have caused much of our grief and sorrow. The God we've been forced to love acts like the ones who abuse and oppress us still. The God we've been required to trust looks like the ones who have betrayed us over and over and over again.

But, we are women of African descent. We know in our very cells that what we see is only half the truth. We know that the pictures and images and words and even actions give only one perspective of reality. We know that our world is also real and that our truth comes from the heart of God.

We will always have struggles with our men. We will forever have difficulties with our children. We will indeed have other rivers we will have to cross. But we don't have to struggle with God any more. That strife can be over—that battle is already won! It's time to lay down, put our heads back, and do a backfloat in the Holy Spirit. We don't have to worry about drowning any more.

Thought for the Day: Backfloat! You will not drown!

Linda Lee is currently the district superintendent of the Detroit East District of the Detroit Annual Conference of the United Methodist Church. Formerly the chair of the Black Clergywomen of the United Methodist Church, she has taught spiritual formation at Ecumenical Theological Seminary in Detroit, Michigan, and numerous workshops on women's spirituality and pastoral care.

Vanessa Stephens Lee

Strange Relationships

Mothers and Their Sons

His mother said to him, "My son, let the curse fall on me. Just do what I say. . . . " —Genesis 27:13 (NIV)

As mothers, women have great power of influence over men. Mothers have the power to help shape their sons into strong, yet lovable men. Or we can shape them into weak, wimpy men who are a hindrance to themselves and to other women.

Rebecca is a prime example of a mother's power to influence. While it may seem that Rebecca took great advantage of her power to influence, she was, in fact, operating in the will of God. She knew that God favored Jacob. So Rebecca used cunning and wit to get Jacob in a position to receive his blessing.

The greatest gift a mother can give to her children, and especially to her sons, is to rear them to be in a position to receive the special blessings God has in store for them. Too often, mothers miss this opportunity by overindulging their sons. As a result, many mothers bring up boys they themselves would not want to marry!

Far too many boys grow up to be adult boys clinging to women who take care of them. It's because their mothers, who were their primary caregivers, never taught them to take care of themselves. Doing for them what they should learn to do for themselves hinders, stunts, retards, and stops their development process.

Consequently, these boys grow up to be men who want women to cater to their every need. Jacob had to learn how to work for his own blessings. In the beginning Rebecca prepared the meal required for Jacob's blessing. Years later, Jacob discovered anything worth having was worth working for and waiting on.

Jacob worked fourteen years for the woman he loved, and another seven to give her and his family security. There was a time when we would hear of "pretty women and hard working men." More often than not, now, we have pretty men and hard working women. That's what we get when we teach our girls to think and fend for themselves and allow our boys to be catered to.

If God has blessed you with a son, or a grandson, rear him to be a man that you would be proud to marry. Teach them to be one who will love God, love himself, and love his family as Christ loved the church. Then, you will have done exceedingly well with the gift that God has given to you. Every child is a gift from God.

Thought for the Day: Train children in the right way, and when old, they will not stray (Proverbs 22:6).

Vanessa Stephens Lee, a graduate of Wesley Theological Seminary, is an ordained minister and senior pastor of the Federalsburg-Denton Charge, United Methodist Churches. She is married to the Reverend David M. Lee, and they are proud parents and grandparents. She is currently matriculating through the Doctor of Ministry program, also at WTS, in Washington, D.C.

Ramonia Lee-Shopshire

Everything Must Change

> *Forget the former things; do not dwell on the past. See, I am doing a new thing! —Isaiah 43:18–19 (NIV)*

Many times in my life I wish that things would stay just like they are. Life can get comfortable—with no waves, just smooth sailing—and then we sense that we are about to experience a major change in the scheme of things. The old song by Quincy Jones tells us that everything must change, nothing stays the same. Change is inevitable. Yet we resist change even when the change may be good for us.

Not only do we resist change; we also ignore God's signs, which signal that the time for change has come. When God indicates it is time to move to a new job or alter our lifestyle, we spend time rationalizing why we should stay put instead of making plans to move forward. When God gives us clear and unmistakable signs to let go of a relationship or to embrace a new calling or to reverse our course and head in a new direction, we stop and question God's leading.

When we resist change, we are resisting God. We are proclaiming that we would rather lean on our own understanding than depend upon the guidance of the all wise God. We are declaring that we choose to follow our own instincts instead of the leading of the all-knowing God.

Each time the Spirit beckons us to change, God is reminding us that we are not yet what we can become. When we are open to moving on— to making a change in our personal, professional, or spiritual lives—that openness becomes an opportunity for us to grow and mature. Change requires that we exercise a measure of faith. Change requires that we let go of our desires in an effort to follow God's directions. Most importantly, change requires that we trust and rely on God.

I have experienced many changes in the last few years. I have moved from ministry with one congregation to ministry in a religious non-profit

organization that works with ninety-seven con-
gregations. I've given up my cherished status as
a single woman to marry for the first time. I
have changed the focus of my ministry from
working with the younger generations to working with elders. Some of these changes have
been welcomed. Some have been difficult. All
have transformed me into the woman God wants
me to be. None of the changes would have been
made, however, without a willingness to trust in
God and the faith to make a move on to a new
venture. Yes, change is inevitable! May we be
willing to risk a new thing with God.

**Thought for the Day: Everything must
change! Change that is from God is
good.**

Ramonia Lee-Shopshire is a program associate with
the Community Ministries program of Baptist Senior
Adult Ministries. She is a graduate of Hampton Institute,
the University of Richmond, and Wesley Theological
Seminary, and she is currently enrolled in the D.Min.
program at Wesley Theological Seminary. Ramonia is
an ordained American Baptist clergywoman.

Mary A. Love

Actions Speak Louder than Words

> *Rejoice always, pray without ceasing, give thanks in all circumstances; for this is the will of God in Christ Jesus for you. —1 Thessalonians 5:16–18 (NRSV)*

How many times has someone made the statement, "Actions speak louder than words"? No doubt you have heard it countless times. I know I have, but it was an experience with my mother that gave a crystal-clear meaning to the phrase. Several years ago, my mother was stricken with a stroke that left her partially paralyzed on one side. After spending a short period of time in the hospital, she was allowed to return home. The paralysis made movement

145

difficult. In the midst of this illness, I learned a lesson and had an indelible image implanted in my mind.

All of my life, I had heard my mother tell me that one should pray at all times. She would readily express her faith in God and constantly witness to the goodness of God and how God had made a way when there appeared to be no way. She would tell of how she had witnessed the hand of God at work in her life as she experienced harsh racist treatment in the Mississippi delta where she had lived since her birth in 1909.

Mother's first day home from the hospital was great for her. She was thankful to God for the return home, and she wanted to do just as she had done before. In spite of the paralysis, she insisted on giving thanks by kneeling by her bedside. She could not kneel or rise without a struggle. But she persisted in kneeling to pray. Her actions gave life to the words of Scripture, when Paul exhorted the believers to "pray without ceasing" (1 Thessalonians 5:17) and "in everything, give thanks" (Ephesians 5:20).

Since that time, my mother has recovered completely from the stroke and has been able to return to many of her favorite activities such as gardening, driving, and doing other tasks around her home. Her practice of praying, showing respect for God, and being gracious to all continues. She has become a role model for me and others as she has fervently modeled the value of prayer and the discipline necessary to obediently pray without ceasing.

How is your prayer life? How dedicated are you to praying without ceasing? Do you find reasons not to pray? Would your actions speak louder than your words if someone observed your prayer life? Would the image of your prayer life have a future impact on an observer in the form of teaching memories?

Thought for the Day: I will examine my prayer life and assess the volume of the message in my actions.

Mary A. Love, editor of church school literature for the African Methodist Episcopal Zion Church, is a graduate of Mississippi State University and Wesley Theological Seminary. She is also adjunct professor of Christian education at Hood Theological Seminary in Salisbury, North Carolina. As an avid writer and dedicated Christian educator, she is constantly working to provide resources to nurture persons in the faith.

Louisa M. Martin

Thirsty

Jesus answered, "Everyone who drinks this water will be thirsty again, but whoever drinks the water I give her will never thirst. Indeed, the water I give her will become in her a spring of water welling up to eternal life." —John 4:13–14 (NIV)

My favorite flavor of Kool-Aid is red. That's right; there is no greater satisfaction on a hot summer day or after a marathon of wearing my superwoman outfit than an ice-cold glass of red Kool-Aid. For me, it is an addiction. I have tried other drinks but to no avail. Red Kool-Aid is it! Thirst can be a funny thing. I can drink any other beverage, but after that initial "aah" and "mmm," the pleasure is short-lived and my thirst is as alive and fresh as when I first attempted to assuage it. And I'm back to red Kool-Aid, feeling a bit annoyed that I wasted time and energy trying to make something else do.

The Samaritan woman had a thirst. And she tried to satisfy it with the several men who had married her and engaged in non-meaningful relationships that had ended in her being divorced and left alone, abandoned. No man in her life would fill that void. None of them could truly satisfy her thirst for intimacy and compassion, her thirst for comfort, her thirst for affirmation, her thirst for acceptance and genuine love. And so we find her at the well, perhaps looking for yet another man. Perhaps a bit put out because she hadn't found the "one" who could and would satisfy—that is until she met Jesus.

The Evangelist John informs us that "Jesus had a need to go through Samaria." Christ went with the purpose of keeping a date with a woman who had an insatiable thirst. In spite of their differences, her needs and past experiences, Jesus showed up knowing that his provision would satisfy her thirst, both internally and eternally. That's a long lasting satisfaction! And she would no longer have to search to satisfy her thirst for the springs of refreshment which were only external and temporary. When comprehension swelled up within her, I can hear her say, "aah" and "mmm"! It was better than red Kool-Aid!

Perhaps your thirst is not for red Kool-Aid. When the pressures and possessions of life make you thirsty for rest, direction, compassion, or help, when you have tried some of everything else to satisfy you, I refer you to the "Well of Living Water," who always satisfies and never runs dry.

Thought for the Day: Lord, my soul thirsts for you. Lead me to your refreshing streams and cause me to drink until I want no more. Spring up, O well, within my soul. Spring up, O well, and make me whole!

Louisa M. Martin, associate pastor of Harvest Fellowship Church in Springfield, Massachusetts, is a preacher, teacher, and humorist. Louisa travels extensively, bringing the Good News throughout the world. She has a special love for both equipping the saints for victory and encouraging her sisters how to "Live Large"!

Rosemary E. Matthews

Growing Through

And the leaves of the tree are for the healing of the nations. —Revelation 22:2 (NRSV)

About fifteen years ago, I worked at a home for multiply-disabled children. The home sat on a wonderful campus with lots of beautiful trees. Every day I would take my morning break, go out and sit on a bench, and have my mid-morning meditation.

After several weeks, I began to notice the individual trees, which seemed to take on their own personalities. They became my sacred space. One trio of trees reminded me of the Trinity, and so I called them my Trinity Trees. Another tree had its arm stretched out horizontally, reminding me of the cross. I named it that.

One day my eyes settled on a huge red maple tree. This tree seemed to have no beginning and no end. I was absolutely stunned by its majesty. Then something else caught my eye. Just under this red maple grew the tiniest evergreen tree. Even after I returned to work, I could not get the image out of my mind. The next day I returned to that bench, and as I looked toward the maple and the little evergreen, I knew why I was so fascinated by them. The red maple tree's wonderful arms seem to surround the little evergreen, protecting it on almost all sides. The little evergreen felt the effects of rain and snow and wind and sun but never in their entirety. Nestled under the red maple, the evergreen could not be blown down or washed away. From its magnificent position, the red maple had watched over the little tree, even preparing a bed for its birth. The evergreen from its position would never know the majestic beneficence of the red maple.

I watched the evergreen as it grew through all the seasons for several years. When cold and snow prevented me from going outside, I went to one of the windows closest to the tree and reflected on it. Once the snow was so high that I worried that the evergreen would be completely covered, but when I looked, there was the evergreen, snow on its branches and around its short trunk and the red maple limbs draped around it.

I have had many winters in these last fifteen years when the ice and cold of circumstances threatened to overcome me, when the winds of oppression and racism would almost knock me down. At those times I have often reflected back to the little evergreen securely resting under the red maple and known that, in the same way, God is sheltering me.

Thought for the Day: I will grow through all the seasons of my life, confident in the knowledge of God's abiding presence.

Rosemary E. Matthews is a mother, grandmother, godmother, aunt, sister, and provider of care of "other people's children." She is a child advocate, a staff member with the Children Sabbath Coalition of Greater Philadelphia, and a charter member of Stand For Children.

Delores E. Lee McCabe

Called

The Queen of the South will rise at the judgment with this generation and condemn it; for she came from the ends of the earth to listen to Solomon's wisdom, and now one greater than Solomon is here. —Matthew 12:42 (NIV)

Jesus Christ encouraged women when he chastised the people of his generation by saying, "The Queen of the South will rise at the judgment with this generation and condemn it; for she came from the ends of the earth to listen to Solomon's wisdom, and now one who is greater than Solomon is here" (Matthew 12:42). Jesus was saying that, because the Queen of the South had judged Solomon correctly, in the final judgment, she would judge this present generation correctly.

Take heart, sisters. An eighty-year-old black male pastor has taken a firm stand on the position of women in the Southern Baptist Convention. And our Lord and Savior Jesus Christ has delegated the role of judge to the black Queen of Ethiopia and Egypt. The Professor/Queen of Sheba formulated the questions; Solomon answered the questions. When he answered, the Professor/Queen of the South graded the exam and gave Solomon an A+. We often talk about the wisdom of Solomon, but we should talk about the wisdom of the Queen of Sheba, too. At the end of her visit with Solomon, she declared, "Praise be to the Lord your God, who has delighted in you and placed you on God's throne to rule for the Lord your God. Because of the love of your God for Israel and God's desire to uphold them forever, you have been made king over them, to maintain justice and righteousness" (2 Chronicles 9:8 NIV).

In that great gettin' up morning, a black woman will judge the people who lived during the time of the historical Jesus! Jesus Christ acknowledged the wisdom of a black woman. If *Christ* called a woman to judge men, women, boys, and girls in the final judgment, why can't twentieth century Christians believe that God has called women to pastor, preach, teach, proclaim, and promote the gospel of Jesus Christ?

My colleague W. Wilson Goode has cited the United Nations as reporting that it will take another thousand years, another millennium before the world stops discriminating against women! Until then, sisters, take heart! God has work for you to do—in this world and in the next world. Keep on working until the day when Jesus Christ returns. Keep on preaching. Keep on teaching. Keep on telling a dying and broken world that Jesus Christ was carried by a woman, delivered to a dying world by a woman, nurtured by a woman, financially supported by women, and lamented over by women, that he suffered and bled like a woman in travail, giving birth to the church. And then women acted as the midwives as they stood around the cross of Calvary watching Jesus Christ as he birthed resurrection life! It is no surprise that women were the last at the cross, the first at the tomb, and the first mandated by Jesus to share the Good News of resurrection.

When the resurrected Christ reached Galilee, "he rebuked the Eleven for their lack of faith and their stubborn refusal to believe those who had seen him after he had risen" (Mark 16:14).

Another way of interpreting this verse is to say, "You should have listened to the women." Women are called, called to preach to a dying world, and those who are lost are called, called to listen to the gospel—even when it is delivered by a woman.

Thought for the Day: Sisters, don't doubt your call!

Dolores E. Lee McCabe is an assistant professor of social justice and counseling and assistant to the provost for multicultural concerns at Eastern College in St. Davids, Pennsylvania. She is the president of the Black American Baptist Caucus and a member of the Association of University Women. Delores has preached in the townships near Johannesburg, Durban, and Cape Town in South Africa, and at an International Youth Conference in the Czech Republic in Eastern Europe.

Trinette V. McCray

Stand Tough

But those who wait for the Lord shall renew their strength.... —Isaiah 40:31 (NRSV)

The closer we get to the new millennium, the more people seem to worry. Instead of enthusiasm rising, anxiety is rising. And the daily news gives us more reasons to be anxious.

I go to work, and my co-workers are anxious. I talk to families and find that mothers, aunts, and grandmas are anxious. Women, men, girls, and boys are anxious about what lies ahead for us. What a terrible thing to go into the Lord's house and find preachers, teachers, choir members, and ushers who are also anxious. Certainly we face challenging times ahead, but we have always faced challenges as women—as mothers, wives, lovers, aunts, grandmothers, sisters, ministers, co-workers, and African American women.

Times past have not been a picnic, that's for sure! Yet, after all that we've been through, God has a word for us today that, as in Isaiah's day, brings both good news and a challenge. Today, my sisters, the good news is that our challenge is not wrapped up in what is going on in our country, our neighborhoods, our homes, or our workplaces. Our challenge is not how we will fare during the tough times. The challenge to us is how *tough* will we stand during the challenging times. Our call is to stand tough—stand tough for God and to stand tough for one another.

One thing we need to do, then, is wait for the Lord. Big sisters are often instructed when rushing out the door, "Wait for your sister!" I'm the youngest, so I know well what role that gave me. Because my sister had been charged not to leave me, I knew that I could do anything and my sister would have to respond. If I slowed up, then my sister would have to slow down; if I stopped paying attention, she would have to talk to me; if I ran ahead of her, she'd have to catch up. Consider those dynamics in our relationship with God! Because we have been charged with waiting on the Lord, we have the responsibility to stay with God.

I have to say that, while it was comforting to have a sister with whom to journey, I was always doubly reassured when walking with Mama. I did not have to be concerned about her leaving me. She was just as interested in keeping up with me as I was in keeping up with her. If I became slack in holding her hand, she'd tighten up her hold on me. When my strength weakened, hers increased. If I began to drift away, she would give a gentle tug. She carried me when I tired and just allowed me to rest a while. Sister, God is like that!

The real gift of this waiting for the Lord is receiving the promise of renewed strength.

Thought for the Day: Today, I will stand tough.

Trinette V. McCray is a native of Milwaukee, Wisconsin. She received her master of religious education degree from Morehouse School of Religion in Atlanta and her D.Min. from Northern Baptist Theological Seminary. She is the vice president of the American Baptist Churches, USA for the 1998–99 biennial and is campus minister at Cardinal Stritch University in Milwaukee.

Barbara J. McFadden

Blessings Cleverly Disguised as Pain

Though my father and mother forsake me, the Lord will receive me. —Psalm 27:10 (*NIV*)

Sometimes blessings may arrive as moments of brokenness. I experienced showers of blessings during a seven-year period while recovering from a failed marriage. In truth the marriage had ended five years before the divorce, but the healing took more time.

"*I need my space!*" Those four words spoken by my former husband literally changed my life forever. Words *do* harm you. They cut as sharply as a surgeon's scalpel. After twenty-one years of marriage and two children later, I became the head of a single-parent family. As a working mom with a professional career, parenting responsibilities for two teenagers—a thirteen-year-old son and an eighteen-year-old daughter—tuition, church obligations, and family of birth obligations, I needed *my* space!

I had not been prepared to become a single parent. Women in our family have an unrelenting commitment to marriage and the family. My failed marriage was a severe indictment against my degree of faith and my relationship/connection with God. My identity as a woman, a mother, a person in my birth family, as an in-law, and as an employee was changed. Every time I heard the words, "I need my space," they gnawed at the very fiber of what I believed was my role as a Christian woman. I was not meant to be a single parent!

The emotional upheaval of divorce plants seeds of destruction within each family member for generations. The hurt and pain of betrayal and mistrust act as fertilizer for generational curses. As a family separated by divorce, we were in hell! I knew that only God could help us. I relied on every precious promise in Scripture. Psalm 27:10 offers a cherished one: "Though my father and mother forsake me, the Lord will receive me."

I was told once during a secular counseling session that if I got myself together then all the ducks would fall in a row. I had been married to marriage and motherhood and lost myself. I had to begin to love and accept myself as a person, a person who needed the same commitment from people as others needed from me. I decided to make *me* the object in a project. I changed my career focus to pastoral counseling, formed a support group for divorced women, read Scripture and wrote in my journal daily, sought ways to improve my spirituality, volunteered at a nursing home during Sunday mass, and monitored my physical health. I had to reconcile my present self with the self God intended for me to become.

Once the effects of these changes began to manifest themselves in my life, I could begin the process of forgiveness. I began by asking forgiveness of my former spouse for the hurt, anger, and pain I caused him. And I told him that I forgave him. We had hurt each other during those twenty-one years, and we had had unrealistic role expectations of each other, although we both came from Christian churchgoing families. During these last few years, we have learned to enjoy each other's company. We have not reconciled as a couple, but we are reconciled enough to be supportive parents to our children, who are now twenty and twenty-five years old.

Surely if I had not sought the Lord during this difficult time, I would not have experienced the joy of healing that reconciliation brings or the liberating feeling of getting to know myself. In truly knowing *who* I am and *whose* I am, I can live the life of the Christian woman the Lord has called me to become. Single or married, I still belong to Christ.

Thought for the Day: Trust in the Lord with all your heart, on your own intelligence rely not; In all your ways be mindful of God who will make straight your paths (Proverbs 3:5–6 NAB).

Barbara J. McFadden is a single mom, registered nurse, legal nurse consultant, and a member of Sacred Heart Roman Catholic Church, Queens, New York, where she serves as a Eucharistic minister. Barb has developed and been involved in programs that have had an impact on Catholics of African descent both nationally and internationally while serving as the director for the Office of Black Catholics for the Diocese of Rockville Centre, New York.

Emma A. Melton

Wouldn't Take Nothin' for My Journey

During my childhood and early adolescence, Sunday morning services were home to a major contradiction in my life. Even before time for the ushers to collect the morning offering, my whole being became anxious. I anticipated receiving the money that I was expected to place in the offering basket—but I was embarrassed by the amount. My family routinely sat together on the second pew in front of the choir. My father, from his position on the aisle, would pass each coin separately to each family member. (My older brother, five years my senior, graduated from the pew and was allowed to sit with friends near the rear of the church.) Humiliation shrouded me as I would pass one nickel each to my younger brothers, accept mine, and watch my mother receive two one dollar bills. Daddy gave one to five dollars.

The "doling out" raised questions about my self-worth, male control of finances, and how to confront. My parents never openly discussed family economics, but my current perception tells me the weekly six to nine dollar contribution exceeded a tithe of my father's wages.

By today's standards, my husband and I do not have the financial safeguards that guarantee future maintenance of our lifestyle. Still, there is money enough to travel, to attend an opera or play, and to volunteer. In reality, I could decide to be *the established*—a member of that elite class called "the establishment." I could focus on budget and investments. A glimpse at my social and academic potential reveal resources that point to "the good life." With my self, my family, and my significant friends as *the priority*, I could develop a maze of possible ways of masking my real problems, real questions, and emerging convictions so that I could "fit in." I could make the status quo my security blanket.

But when I remember the usher holding the offering basket until Daddy doled out our money, I settle in with *the disestablished*. When I visualize my mother lengthening her hand-me-down skirt by crudely sewing an odd piece of fabric to the waistline, I settle in with those who lack financial and social security. When I listen to the frustrations of "at-risk youth" or recall standing in a dung hut in India staring at the soiled strips of gauze that cast a newborn's twisted limbs, I settle in with the disestablished.

In doing so, I'm responding to God's call. As I honor the reality of the abiding grace of God throughout my life, I acknowledge that I've been shepherded by a loving family, by an international cadre of those who care, by spiritual growth groups, by at-risk teens, and by God's own beautiful earth. I've been pruned by disappointment, illness, and episodes of gloomy nights of my soul. I've been called to serve in the most diverse, global/local, and meaningful situations in both church and in community.

Yes, I've settled in with the disestablished, but in reality, I'm wealthy! I'm filthy rich and consequently bold enough to call myself "transestablished." I am a servant leader who prays for perpetual spiritual growth and who designs and facilitates strategies and conversations between the most unlikely groups in order that full community emerges as a hope-filled process.

Thought for the Day: The search for answers to "How shall I think about God?" and "Who am I being?" are key to celebrating this day's journey.

Emma A. Melton received the 1998 Martin L. King, Jr. Ecumenical Award for multiple services rendered to the communities of which she is a part. Her years of research with the Ecumenical Institue and the Institute of Cultural Affairs, International, created numerous facilitation opportunities with organizations that include The Anti-Defamation League, the IERO in New Delhi, India, the Ohio Drug Summit, the Black Education Conference of the American Baptist Churches, USA, and the U.N.-sponsored Fourth World Conference on Women that was held in China.

La Sandra Melton-Dolberry

Confident in Christ

The One who began a good work in you will carry it on to completion.
—Philippians 1:6 (NIV)

"Lord, take me and use me and please don't refuse me, for surely there's a work that I can do. And, though I may seem humble, please help my will to crumble, and I'll work for you." As I drove home from delivering my son to his work and my daughter to school, I started to sing a morning song of worship. I began to feel the presence of God's overwhelming love.

I could plainly see how a loving Creator continuously blessed me but, moreover, how the Lord continuously used me and the gifts bestowed upon me—in spite of me! Other people may marvel at what I do and think how gifted and anointed I must be, but although they may be right in their thinking, they don't have a clue to the great measure of mercy and grace that has been and is yet being imparted to me. Sometimes when I see the wondrous power of God in my life, working through the ministry entrusted to me, I instantly fall on my face—even in the most seemingly inopportune places. Location makes no difference; in my spirit I am bowing before Almighty God, worshiping the beauty of God's mysterious glory. I am more than thankful for the Ancient of Days' unmerited love for me.

Of course, other mornings I wake up face-to-face with Ms. Discouragement. When the adversary of our souls begins to recount all the failures of my past week, I can hear clearly the suggestion, "Quit now, while you're ahead!" But then a voice louder and clearer speaks to my heart and says, "My dear little one, don't ever forget that the One who began a good work in you is able to complete it!" (Philippians 1:6, paraphrased). I am more than thankful for the Holy Spirit's reminder that I really can do all things through Christ who strengthens me!

So with that thought, I get up renewed, refreshed, refocused, and refueled to go out into the hedges and the highways, knowing that I am not self-appointed nor self-assigned. I do, however, look myself in the mirror, take myself by my dress collar, place the forefinger of my right hand in the middle of my own chest and serve notice to myself, one more time! I have no time for self-sympathy and definitely no time to second-guess the wisdom of my God. Like it or not, in following Christ's example, I have been appointed to preach the gospel to the meek, to bind up the brokenhearted, to proclaim liberty to those held captive, and to open prison doors to them that are bound! Therefore, I remain confident of this one thing—if God began it, God can and will perform it, in me and through me. That's how God works! Accomplishing the task is God's business, not mine. My only business is to trust and obey the Omnipotent One. In light of that . . . *look out world! Here I come!*

Thought for the Day: What a privilege to serve the One who will use me, even in my imperfection. You need somebody, Lord? I'm right here. Send me. I'll go!

La Sandra Melton-Dolberry, a native of San Antonio, Texas, is a licensed minister who has worked in various ministries for fifteen years. She is founder of Harambee Urban Ministries, The Gathering Place. Although she functions in full-time ministry, she also works as a community educator and youth advocate. Her passions are pastoral care for women, praise and worship, and urban ministry.

Yvette Moore

Don't Panic

In returning and rest you shall be saved; in quietness and in trust shall be your strength. —Isaiah 30:15b (NRSV)

A while back there was a popular poster that featured a very calm-looking guerrilla soldier sitting in a tree and words that said, in effect, "If you're not panicking, you don't fully understand the situation."

Panic. Fear. Worry. These can all be quite rational responses for anyone who consumes mass media news reports on any regular basis—or for the sister who looks up from her myriad tasks long enough to consider an employment offer, family issues, health concerns, or other situations in her life that she knows are volatile, but over which she alone has little control. What are we to do when the voice of terror screams, "Do *something!*"?

That was the situation in which Judah found itself during the days of Isaiah. Read Isaiah 30. The mighty Assyrian empire had already swallowed the Northern Kingdom of Israel, and Judah knew it was next. Panicked, Judah turned even further away from God on a mission of self-preservation that included a string of bad decisions—which I'm sure at the time seemed pragmatic, even prudent. Judah used oppression and deceit to secure its position; it formed an unholy alliance with Egypt against Assyria. Isaiah proclaimed that, instead of fixing the problem, Judah had piled "sin upon sin." After all was said and done, Judah was in even more trouble than it was before it enacted its survival plan.

Panic-driven responses to life's challenges can lead to decisions that we long regret. What to do, what to do? Resist the call to panic; the answer is not there anyway. Today, hear Isaiah's good word from the Lord: *The Lord waits to be gracious to you; therefore, God will rise up to show mercy to you. For the Lord is a God of justice; blessed are all those who wait for the Lord.* (Isaiah 30:18 NRSV)

Thought for the Day: I won't panic because I do not understand the situation; I know that God is in control, waiting to be gracious to me.

Yvette Moore is managing editor of *Response*, the magazine of United Methodist Women. She is the author of a young-adult novel, *Freedom Songs* (1991) and the author/publisher of *The Birth of Christ* (1993), a colorful multicultural rendition of the Christmas story for children. She is a wife and mother of two.

Daniela Y. Morrisey

God Is Moving

For surely I know the plans I have for you, says the Lord, plans for your welfare and not for harm, to give you a future with hope. —Jeremiah 29:11 (NRSV)

God is always moving in our lives. God is always calling us to live in our potential, beyond what we see. God is challenging us to be all we can be. God has a purpose for each one of us, a purpose that is for our good.

An old church song says, "How I got over. How I got over. My soul looks back and wonders, how I got over." The words remind me of my calling into professional ministry. When I look back, I can see God moving. I can see the Spirit preparing and leading me into ministry.

But while I was going through, I was just trying to make it, day by day.

I remember desiring more from life than just
the trappings of temporal bliss. I remember
thinking, if I get all the material things I want,
then what? Will I just want more? Will I ever
be satisfied?

So then I asked myself, what really matters
most? Is it money? When you die, you can't take
it with you. Is it power? Someone is always trying to unseat the person at the top. Is it fame?
Just as quickly as you are loved you can be
hated. And then I heard the words of another
song: "Only what you do for Christ will last."

I came to realize that our relationships are
more important than anything, in particular our
relationships with God and each other. Images
of these will last. They are what life is all about.
Moreover, through this revelation about relationships, I heard God's call. I sensed God saying to me, "Tell this to my people. Teach my
people who I am and what's really important in
life."

In looking back, I saw God moving, calling
me into my purpose, my vocation. I was unable
to recognize God's actions while I was in the
midst of my situation. But now I know God is

always moving in all of our lives. God desires the best for all of us, which involves coming to a more intimate knowledge of God. Turn your ear and attention to the Lord. What awaits you is far greater than anything you can imagine or dream.

Thought for the Day: Lord, help us to hear and answer your call. Amen.

Daniela Y. Morrisey is the minister of Christian education and special projects at the St. Paul Baptist Church in Montclair, New Jersey. She is a graduate of Rutgers University and Princeton Theological Seminary.

Karen E. Mosby-Avery

Scarred

So Jacob called the place Peniel, say-ing, "For I have seen God face to face, and yet my life is preserved." The sun rose upon him as he passed Penuel, limping because of his hip. —Genesis 32:30–31 (NRSV)

When I look in the mirror these days, I can see three scars on my body that are visible re-minders of my journey over the last decade. As the light hits each of them, they take me into the presence of God.

The first scar is the "bikini cut" that I received when my twins were born via cesarean section. No one else can see the scar, and most of the time I don't think about it. But then, out of nowhere a slight ache or irritation around the scar will bring back memories of the pain and the joy that accompanied my children's birth. I can remember the anxious moments of wondering if they would be healthy, if I would be a good mother, if I could love them as they deserved to be loved. I recall how alone I felt as I waited to be wheeled into the operating room, wrapped in warmed blankets and watching people pass by as though nothing out of the ordinary was about to happen. When I gaze at this scar, I remember the faithfulness of God who promised that the "fruit" of my womb would be blessed.

The second scar was left after the removal of a benign lump from my right breast. When I look at it, I think about the fear that overpowered my faith when it was discovered. Here I was, a mother of twins, a pastor, a woman of God, and all I could think about then was not being around to share in my children's life. It wasn't that I couldn't remember the words I had given others who were in similar situations. But in that space I felt estranged from the words of faith. What if they found a malignancy? What if I only had a few more months to live? And of course I asked, "Why me?" God continues to minister to me through this scar, especially when I have aligned myself with fear. This scar reminds me that I must daily choose: "Will I trust God or not?"

Unlike the first two scars that are hidden from the public eye, the third one appears noticeably as a dark, ragged line across my neck. Every Sunday as I stand up to preach, it stands up with me. I cannot avoid seeing it, nor can others. When I was told that a cyst on my thyroid had to be removed, the news did not evoke fear. I'm not one who spiritualizes everything, but I was persuaded that this surgery was more than a medical procedure. Often God chooses to operate in unexpected ways. God allows things to happen in order to direct our attention toward a "greater work" that is being done. When I touch my neck, I can feel God's touch and hear the words, "Be still and know that I am God."

When I fill out medical forms that ask about surgical procedures, I list my three. But there is never enough space to tell the whole story—not just the dates and what was removed, but God's activity. As I stand at the mirror facing my scars, sometimes I imagine that Jacob is standing alongside me, favoring one side of his body over the other after being disfigured in his divine wrestling match. We both smile, and I celebrate yet another renaming. Today, I dance and call myself "Scarred." For through my scars, I have met God and have been forever *trans*figured.

Thought for the Day: My scars are visible and tangible evidence of God's presence in my life.

Karen E. Mosby-Avery currently serves as a pastor at the Good News Community Church in Chicago, Illinois. In addition, she has worked as a program consultant for the Center for the Church and the Black Experience at Garrett-Evangelical Theological Seminary in Evanston, Illinois. She is the mother of twins, Ayo and Issa.

Gale Kennebrew Poindexter

Check Your Switch!

> *Yours, O Lord, is the greatness and the power and the glory and the majesty and the splendor, for everything in heaven and earth is yours. . . . In your hands are strength and power to exalt and give strength to all.* —1 Chronicles 29:11–12 (NIV)

My son Matthew was trying to play a tape on his boom box, and for some reason the tape player was not working. Matthew plugged the tape player into the electrical outlet in his sister's bedroom—and the tape didn't work. Then he went into his brother's bedroom and tried the outlets there. The tape didn't work. He tried in the bathroom, the kitchen, the living room—and not one of them worked.

Finally, Matthew brought his boom box into the den where I was reading and plugged the tape player in. It still didn't work. He sighed, "Mom, I thought for sure this tape player would work in here!"—in spite of the fact that it had not worked in any of the other rooms in the house.

I looked at my son and saw myself and countless others who are frustrated and confused about their lack of power from time to time. God was speaking to me through my son's frustration. I said to him, "Matthew, the same power source that runs into this room runs into each and every room throughout the entire house." Then I looked closely at the power switch on the tape player. When I wiggled it, I found that there was a short in the wiring. Nothing was wrong with the electricity—there was a short in the switch.

Are you living with the death of a loved one?

Wondering where you're going to get enough money to pay your bills?

Caring for aging parents?

Burnt out?

Doctor can't find the source of your pain?

A child caught up in gangs and drugs?

Spouse cheating in the next room?

Have you lost your job?

Lost your passion, your focus, and your sense of purpose?

Are you wondering why you do not have power? Don't blame God . . . check your switch!

The same God that promised Sarah also promised Hagar. The same God that blessed your neighbor will bless you. The same God that healed the woman with the issue of blood will heal you. The same God that freed Mandela will free you. The same God that restored Job will restore you. The same God that provided for the multitude will provide for you. The same God that raised Lazarus will raise you. The same God that delivered me will deliver you!

Thought for the Day: Take courage. . . . Check your switch. *The Power is still on!*

Gale Kennebrew Poindexter is a native of Chicago, Illinois. She is presently serving as vice president of religion and health at South Suburban Hospital in Hazel Crest, Illinois. She is a United Church of Christ minister, is married to Kent, and has three children.

Anita Adams Powell

A Message from the E-ZPass

I am the way. . . . —John 14:6 (NIV)

Recently, I visited a family where the thirty-eight-year-old daughter was dying. As I was leaving, the mother hurriedly came downstairs and said, "My daughter wants me to give you her E-ZPass. She said, 'Mom, give the E-ZPass to Anita so that she can use it to cross over and go through the tolls. Tell her to be careful on the road. It's rough out there. Hurry, Mom, before she leaves.'"

The E-ZPass is a device that, when mounted on the inside of a car, allows access to toll bridges and roads without having to pay cash each time one crosses. This ordinary, simple, and practical device, which was offered as a special gift for safe passage across roads of life, deeply intrigued me.

As soon as I arrived home, I looked at the E-ZPass. On it was written: "E-ZPass; Property of New York State Thruway Authority; P.O. Box 189, Albany, New York; For Customer Service, call 1-800-222-8655; Return Postage Guaranteed." Then it was marked with an identifying serial number.

I sensed something mystical and supernatural about this, something that was not of the flesh, but of the Holy Spirit. So instead of placing the E-ZPass on my souvenir shelf, I placed it on my prayer altar. For I believed that there was a message in the E-ZPass.

The E-ZPass speaks to me about being the "property of." The reality is that we belong to God, who has a claim on our lives. Each of us has a name tag with an "identifying number," making us unique and special to God. This is a message from the E-ZPass.

E-ZPass speaks to me about "authority." Jesus has the power and the authority to exercise control over our coming and our going. For his ordering of our steps, we should give thanks and glory to God. This is a message from the E-ZPass.

E-ZPass speaks to me about "customer service." We are the customers of life, and Jesus came to provide us with divine service. He takes our requests, gives us directions, listens to our complaints, resolves our problems, and specializes in our consumer protection. This is a message from the E-ZPass.

E-ZPass speaks to me of toll-free, unlimited access, a 1-800 hotline of open communication that is available twenty-four hours a day. Whenever we need to talk to someone, there is One who answers our call. The phone is listed in the Name of Jesus whose shed blood covers all charges and costs. This is a message from the E-ZPass.

E-ZPass speaks to me of "return postage guaranteed." This world is not our home, and as visitors, we each have a round-trip ticket; our return postage is guaranteed. Death is actually our final return trip home. This is a message of the E-ZPass.

E-ZPass speaks to me about a return mailing address. This reminds me that God has already established for us an eternal residence in a "new" place. Heaven will be our birthplace into everlasting life. This is a message from the E-ZPass.

Finally, the E-ZPass speaks to me about a "thruway." As we change our place of residence, we must have a way of getting there. We are reminded that Jesus is the Way through whom all who believe may be saved. Through the hands of one who was dying—transitioning, moving from this life to life eternal, the message came through, loud and clear to me, that Jesus is *the* E-ZPass! Thanks be unto God!

Thought for the Day: We thank you, God, for sending Jesus, our E-ZPass, to carry us across the highways and by-ways and over the bridges of troubled waters into a new life, giving us unlimited access to hope and peace. Amen.

Anita Adams Powell is an ordained minister of American Baptist Churches, U.S.A., who serves as the associate director of admissions and adjunct professor of Christian ministries at the Eastern Baptist Theological Seminary. She is a Benjamin E. Mays Scholar who received her B.S. from Hampton University, her M.A. from Wesleyan University (Connecticut), and her M.Div. from the Eastern Baptist Theological Seminary. She serves on the ministerial staff at St. Paul's Baptist Church in West Chester, Pennsylvania.

Jocelyn M. Roper

Reshaping Broken Vessels

> *So I went down to the potter's house, and there he was working at his wheel. The vessel he was making of clay was spoiled in the potter's hand, and he reworked it into another vessel, as seemed good to him. —Jeremiah 18:3–4 (NRSV)*

Two years ago, my supervisor asked me if I would consider reclaiming my passion for working with youth. Prayer and several life events affirmed for me that youth ministry was the labor to which God was calling me. I began working with youth in the local area, as well as across the state and around the nation. I planned and attended youth conferences; I led workshops for and with youth; I preached to youth.

Many times, at the close of these events, I felt physically exhausted but emotionally exhilarated and spiritually energized by the openness and the willingness of the youth to be shaped by the power of the Holy Spirit.

Things went well with my ministry until February 2, 1998, the day my mother died. While I grieved then and still grieve for her, I recognized that her death was a blessed release for her as she slipped quietly into the arms of God. She had had an intense battle with cancer for the last four years of her life, and we all went through it with her. My children were devastated by her death. They had been "her children" just as Ruth's son Obed became Naomi's own. Four of the five children were able to express their grief. My youngest daughter, Jeannetté, was not.

Jeannetté sought answers for the pain she was feeling from adults she loved and respected, but she found little help. As I learned later, her pain grew so intense that she began cutting herself to "stay in touch with the fact that she was real."

I was devastated when I discovered this. I was in ministry with youth, but I had missed her cries for help! I was further dismayed because I did not have adequate training to help her deal with the depths of her despair. But thank God, I had the sense to put my feelings aside and get my child the help she needed.

Things did *not* get better. While the cutting stopped, her ability to cope—with school and with the people there who had hurt her badly—seemed on a continual downward spiral. I began to realize that the institution that was supposed to help this child in learning about life, the system that she and I had trusted to assist in molding and shaping her young mind, was causing her demise.

Like Jeannetté, I felt betrayed. I withdrew her from public school, and with the help of my husband and my middle son, Jesse, we began the process of home-schooling Jeannetté. Her healing began.

Jeannetté started in a new school in August. While she still suffers the ups and downs of thirteen-year-olds, she has made amazing progress. She now seeks ways in which she can help extended family members and me, especially if she feels we are in pain. She realizes the importance of prayer, and she acknowledges and appreciates the fact that many people were praying for her during her times of struggle. She finds comfort and strength in evening Bible study and the devotional time that she spends with her twin brother, Jared, and with me. She is, and is becoming, a beautiful new vessel.

In Jeremiah 18:1–4, when the object that the potter was shaping developed a crack, the potter did not discard it but gently, compassionately, and lovingly reworked the clay into a beautiful new vessel, a new creation. The vicissitudes of life often leave us cracked and broken! If we are willing to be remolded, reshaped, renewed, restored, re-created, and even redeemed by a loving, caring, compassionate, and empathetic Potter, we too may come forth as wondrous and awesome people.

As we speak and act with a prophetic voice against the systems, powers, and evil of this world, we are assured that God has the creative and redemptive power to put us, our children, our youth, and even this broken and fractured world back together again.

Thought for the Day: As mothers, sisters, aunts, daughters, we are the ones who have borne the pain and agony of our people. But we are also the ones to give birth to faith, hope, and possibility. God invites us to participate in the process of reshaping imperfect and broken vessels.

Jocelyn M. Roper is the wife of Jesse and mother of Joshua, Jesse II, Jasmine, Jared, and Jeannetté. She is the associate director for Youth and Missional Ministries in the West Ohio Conference of the United Methodist Church. She works with youth from diverse cultures, has served as a consultant for many national youth events, and is co-director of People Under Construction, a life-changing vehicle for shaping the life of youth for leadership.

Jini Kilgore Ross

Melodies from the Maker

Hear my cry, O God; attend unto my prayer. From the end of the earth will I cry unto thee, when my heart is overwhelmed: lead me to the rock that is higher than I. For you have been a shelter for me. . . . —Psalm 61:1–3 (NKJV)

A favorite song in my church during my girlhood was based on Psalm 61. The refrain was, "Lead me to the rock that is higher than I; Higher than I; Oh, higher than I; Lead me to the rock that is higher than I; Thou hast been a shelter for me" (Traditional). Forty years later, I never hear those scriptural words of supplication without also hearing their accompanying melody, so this simple refrain has become one of the staple songs of my heart.

Songs like this one linger lovingly underneath my conscious thoughts, often without my immediate notice, faithfully playing over and over until at last I turn my attention to them. Once I finally stop to listen, I am blessed by a waiting balm that soothes my fretful nerves. I receive a word of assurance that fortifies my failing courage. I delight in a joyful verse that celebrates my small victories. And, I hear a right-on-time answer to my half-muttered prayers.

From the ends of the earth, God hears our cries and commands heaven's music to play melodies in our hearts that will speak peace to us. The psalmist wrote, "And in the night God's song shall be with me" (Psalm 42:8 KJV).

Spiritual music is a divine medium that transports God's presence, love, and care to us. Are you listening for your song?

Thought for the Day: We plant melodic seeds that will ripen to bless others in their times of need when we continue "speaking to one another in psalms, hymns, and spiritual songs, singing and making melody in our hearts to the Lord" (Ephesians 5:19 NASV).

Jini Kilgore Ross is founding co-pastor of New Vision Baptist Church of Katy, Texas; instructor of English composition at Houston Community College Northwest Campus; and a writer and editor. She recently co-authored with her father, the late Dr. Thomas Kilgore, Jr., *A Servant's Journey: The Life and Work of Thomas Kilgore* (Judson Press).

Kim Martin Sadler

Let No Man Write My Epitaph

I'm not saying you must marry; but you certainly may if you wish. I wish everyone could get along without marrying, just as I do. But we are not all the same. God gives some the gift of a husband or wife, and others God gives the gift of being able to stay happily unmarried. So I say to those who aren't married, and to widows—better to stay unmarried if you can, just as I am. —1 Corinthians 7:6–8 (TLB)

Let No Man Write My Epitaph is the title of one of my favorite movies. Starring Lana Turner, the movie is about male/female relationships. What I liked most about this movie is that Turner grew to become a strong, determined woman who knew what she wanted and how she should get it—all without solely depending on a man. Now you might wonder where I am going with this story. In the past few months, I have had more and more of my single female friends ask me for advice about men.

First of all, let me make myself perfectly clear. I love men. I am a happily married woman and the mother of a son. Yet I can remember my "living single" days. Because of this, my friends seek my advice when they are concerned about their "singleness." As some of you know, the issue of being a single African American woman is serious business!

My friends are attractive, intelligent, and gainfully employed. Some are single parents. They own their own homes, drive luxury cars, have substantial stock portfolios, and enjoy annual vacations. However, even with these assets, they do not feel whole—because they are single and they want to get married. Unfortunately, my friends believe that they have little self-worth because of their marital status. Now they are "waiting to exhale," and like Stella, they want to get their "groove back!"

Let's look at Paul's first letter to the Corinthians to address this matter. In chapter 7, verses 6–7 we find: "I'm not saying you *must* marry; but you certainly *may* if you wish. I wish everyone could get along without marrying, just as I do. But we are not all the same. God gives some the gift of a husband or wife, and others God gives the gift of being able to stay happily unmarried."

Paul understands that not everyone can live alone and maintain a celibate life as he does. Too often, my friends lament about lacking "that special someone in their lives." I understand the importance of this and don't underestimate their concerns. However, one of our downfalls as women is viewing every man we meet as a "potential husband." If someone gives a friend of mine a compliment, he becomes her "potential husband." If someone invites her out to dinner, that person becomes a "potential husband." Most of my friends are so busy worrying about a husband that they cannot foster positive platonic relationships with men. As women, we must first develop a friendship with a man. For that matter, nothing is wrong with having several male friends as companions.

I once heard a preacher say that, in order for a person to be *happily unmarried*, "they must find their oneness with God." In other words, we each need to focus our attentions on finding out God's purpose and intention for our lives. In the process of that searching, all that God has for us will come to us. We need to recognize that, with God, we are whole persons with immense possibilities and innumerable capabilities. The real challenge that my single friends face is not in finding a man but in finding a focus and a direction. We as women, both single and married, must never forget that our self-worth and personhood are not measured by the man with whom we are in relationship but rather by the One who claims us and on whose name we call.

Thought for the Day: Sisters, we must move from desperation to deliverance; from emptiness to empowerment; and from loneliness to the light of God's love.

Kim Martin Sadler is the acquisitions editor for United Church Press. She is the editor of *Atonement: The Million Man March* and of the annual devotional book, *The Book of Daily Prayer, Morning and Evening.* She is a wife and mother who loves her girlfriends!

Deborah L. Shumake, Jà Phia

I Am Praying for My Sisters and My Sisters Are Praying for Me

Confess your faults to one another, and pray one for another, that ye may be healed. —James 5:16 (KJV)

This *soul sistering* began for me just before I entered that place known as trials and tribulations. Before then, my up-close and personal friends were actually males. Perhaps I had bought into society's myths about the integrity of women—you know, those myths that say women can't be trusted, or that two women can't be in the same kitchen. While I'm not sure why I had no relationships with women, the grace of God stretched my relationships so that I would have sister friends to support me. After all, God thought so much of women that the Savior of the world was implanted in a woman's womb. God trusted her to receive, carry, nurture, and deliver the *Best* to the world. Women are special!

In April of 1976, my world began caving in. Twenty-seven years old with five small children, I entered the realm of life called testings. My head and my heart were confused. My marriage was over. My second son, Severin Trevor, drowned in a backyard swimming pool during a church function. No Severin, no husband, no finances, no job, and I was on the border of a nervous breakdown. I now weighed about 75 pounds. My oldest son, who was nine at the time, put his fingers around my ankles, exclaiming, "Mama, you must be sick! Look how little your legs are."

My love emotions battled for clarity as well. Love had walked into my life while I was legally married to another. Because I had been a teacher of the scriptures since age nine, I knew God's Word, and I could not feel comfortable in the relationship. I prayed, "God, what do you want me to do? " God had always answered me. But, I had confused myself. I was afraid—afraid that God might say *no* and afraid that God might say *yes*. I wasn't ready for either answer. I was truly a mess—sorrowful and bewildered.

During our Friday Night Cabaret for Jesus, I was directed to one of the new converts. I said in my own heart, "She doesn't know anything, and therefore, her prayers will be pure and clear." I walked up to this babe in Christ, and I said to her, "Do you believe in Jesus?" She answered, "Yes." I said, "Do you love Jesus?" She said, "Yes." I said, "Do you love me?" She said, "Yes." Then I said to her, "I am so confused about my life. Would you pray and ask God to show you what I am to do?" Trembling and afraid because she had never prayed to God for a direct answer, she said, "Yes." Three days later, she shared a vision that changed my entire life.

That experience did at least three things. First, my sister friend developed her own faith walk with God. Second, I learned that when I am in doubt, God will provide wisdom through others. Thirdly, I understood that love's greatest aim is to bless the object of that love. When my sister friend prayed for me out of her love for

God and for me, we both received from the Fountain of Love.

Today, I am partnering with God to bring esteem and harmony to the lives of women because of sisters who have consistently prayed for me. Twenty-three years later, through good times and through bad times, I am praying for my sisters and my sisters are praying for me.

Thought for the Day: Lord, thank you for the woman-power of being able to receive life, to carry life, to nurture life, to deliver life, and to empower life through you.

Deborah L. Shumake, Jà Phia, is a preacher of the gospel. She is the CEO and publisher of *God's Woman Magazine*, a magazine for women who love and serve Jesus Christ. Deborah also owns GWP, Inc., a commercial printing/media consortium in Detroit, Michigan.

Claudette E. Sims

A Picture of Obedience

Here am I, send me! —Isaiah 6:8
(*NRSV*)

Several years ago, before I announced my
call to the ministry, I was visiting a church in
downtown Houston that ministers to the homeless. Fifteen men and women came forward during the call for discipleship, but the pastor felt
that there was one more person struggling with
this life-changing decision.

As if on cue, the Holy Spirit said to me,
"There's a young man on the pew behind you.
Turn around and give him a hug." But almost as
quickly, Satan tried to make me ignore that still,
quiet voice. "Suppose the young man doesn't
respond to your gesture and you look foolish?

Homeless people usually smell like alcohol and urine. Did you really want to hug him? Let somebody else do it," Satan whispered. "It's not even your church!"

But the Holy Spirit is persistent. After all, wasn't I the one who was always asking, "Lord, what will you have me to do?" I felt enveloped in the presence of God, and again I heard the Holy Spirit say, "Be obedient. Turn around and hug that young man!"

Thank God that greater is the Loving One in me than the one who is in the world! I turned around and beckoned to the young man. He leaned across the pew and fell into my open arms without saying a word. And then, as if I were listening from a distance, I heard myself say, "God asked me to give you a hug this morning and to tell you that the Lord can fix anything!"

I started to cry and quickly turned around. But I immediately felt a hand on my shoulder. It was the woman seated next to the young man. She smiled at me as I turned around, and together we watched him head down the aisle. I started to cry uncontrollably and thought my legs might collapse. But God had other plans. As soon as the young man stood before the congregation, he looked back at me and smiled. That smile was my reward. God wanted me to see what obedience looked like!

I marvel at what the Holy Spirit *can* and *will* do if we are open, receptive, and obedient. We must never stop thanking God for the power and prompting of the Holy Spirit and the opportunity to be an instrument for our Creator. If we truly want to grow in Christ and be used by God, we must move "us" out of the way and keep the channel of our spirits clear of fear, doubt, and insecurity. And, we must trust in the power of the Holy Spirit to bring those things to pass which God has purposed in our lives and in the lives of those we touch.

Thought for the Day: Keep my heart open to your voice, Lord, and my eyes open to see what obedience looks like!

Claudette E. Sims is a member of the clergy team at Wheeler Avenue Baptist Church in Houston, Texas. She is also a former television and radio talk show host, a motivational speaker, playwright, poet, and author of three books including her latest, *Loving Me*, for single African American women (February 1999).

Tara R. Sutton

Revival in the Land

Will you not revive us again, so that your people may rejoice in you?
—Psalms 85:6 (NRSV)

It was the first time in a long time that this church had a revival. Yet, the people asked for a revival. They were excited about the whole idea. I explained to the committees that revival meant to bring back to life and to restore us again. After an explanation of revival, it was decided by two committees that a revival must occur because our church was in need of it.

The theme was "Rejoice!" It was scheduled for a weekend and because I was the new pastor, I was asked to be the preacher for revival. The church was filled with much excitement as the weekend of revival approached. We made great efforts to evangelize the community and the city about revival.

The first night of revival, we began to worship the Lord in a new way. Everyone seemed to be on fire for the Lord. The Holy Spirit was alive in the house as we began to magnify the Lord in praise songs, testifying of God's goodness, mercy, and grace. There is deliverance in the praise. After everyone left that night, my cousin and I continued to praise the Lord.

The next night came. As we returned for revival, I was still expecting to see the move of God. However, as I entered into worship that evening I experienced an attack against the revival worship services. Someone did not understand this move of God.

Unfortunately, I almost let the devil steal my joy. Instead of focusing on the fact that God had answered my prayer of having a great revival, I concentrated on the negative words that I heard. I shared some of those issues with my husband and other close friends after the service. They offered words of encouragement, reminding me that the devil always gets angry when we are doing a new work for the Lord.

After the revival, I took some time to reflect on what happened that weekend. First, God sent me some help, people who understood revival to participate, pray, and support this effort. Secondly, I remembered when we go all out for God by praying, fasting, winning souls, and praising God, we will face opposition from the enemy of our souls. Thirdly, the revival in the land was a great success despite Satan's best efforts. The Lord reminded me of who had called for revival in the land! Many people came from different churches to be revived again. God restored many lives. My own spirit was refreshed with those services. Finally, I am assured that God received the victory, for the breaking down of strongholds did occur as we celebrated and rejoiced in our God.

Thought for the Day: Remember, let us not be moved by the circumstances that try to hinder the move of God. Remain focused. Your "help comes from the Lord . . ."

Tara R. Sutton is the pastor of Oak Park United Methodist Church. A member of the Detroit Annual Conference, she is a former consultant-trainer for Urban Outreach Ministries, an African American Sunday school literature distributor. Ordained in the African Methodist Episcopal Church, Tara is a wife and mother.

Sandra L. Swans

Meeting Storms of Life

> *Great is the Lord, who delights in the welfare of God's servant. —Psalm 35:27 (NRSV)*

This passage from the Psalms is on the wall directly in front of my desk. I cannot sit in my chair and not see this quote. Since I met Georges, the hurricane, on the tiny island of Antigua, however, this scripture is not just on paper; it is a part of my very being.

Without thought of checking to see if a hurricane or tropical storm was in the Atlantic, my cousin and I decided on rather short notice to take a late summer break. How delightful, we thought, to get away to the warm waters of the Caribbean and relax completely for three days or so. After we made the decision, everything went like clockwork. No problems with reservations, seats, delays at airports, hassles with baggage. In fact, when we arrived, I proudly announced to our host this was definitely a smooth trip. My cousin reminded me that even the airline reservation clerk had remarked that "this was a trip meant to be because there is absolutely no problem with these reservations at such short notice."

Less than twenty-four hours later, the announcement came of Hurricane Georges' expected arrival. Its first landfall, as a category four storm, was scheduled by morning. The airport had already closed, so there was no way out. *This* was a time to pray. My prayers were answered with quiet calm. As we moved about making hurricane preparations, I had a still, quiet assurance that all was well. In fact, the still, quiet voice in my spirit constantly repeated, "I have not abandoned you ever. Look for the lesson."

When the winds started to rage high and we took our appointed place in the hallway on pillows, in quiet prayer I asked again for protection but also for revelation. I wanted to know what the Lord would teach me through this experience. After four hours of winds, the eye of the storm began to pass. What calm, what peace. I was awed by the wonder that, after all the fury of the winds, such calm could come so suddenly. One hour later the eye completed its passage, and for five hours more, the winds and rains raged. Each approaching wind had a different sound. And then there came rain with no winds. The danger of the storm was over. We were safe and sound, not even wet.

The lesson was clear. God calls us into the eye of the storms of our lives. The storms will come. They will come strong with great rage. But, in the midst of the fury is the eye where we find complete calm and peace. Our prayer is not for storms to stay away. In the movement of the universe, they must come. We, however, need not be the wind and the rage of the storm. We can be the eye, which is calm and peace.

Thought for the Day: The Lord's delight is upon you today—so you may be at peace!

Sandra L. Swans, a native of Philadelphia, Pennsylvania, is a consultant, trainer, meeting planner, and photographer with the General Board of Global Ministries of the United Methodist Church. She lives in New York.

Deborah Tinsley Taylor

Blessed Are the Pure in Heart

Blessed are the pure in heart, for they will see God. —Matthew 5:8 (NRSV)

The definitive statement of human perfection has to be "Ivory Soap is 99.44 percent pure." I remember this line from a television commercial that was broadcast during the soap operas in the 1950s, when I was a child. Of course, my family were dutiful consumers and bought the product. We used it for bathing and laundry, and I always wondered what would it take to be 100 percent pure. However not being perfect didn't have much meaning for me at that time.

Then I found Jesus and realized what *I* was! Christ's words in Scripture began to matter a lot

214

to me. When Jesus said, "Blessed are the pure in heart," I felt sorrowful, excluded, bereft. Jesus could not possibly have meant this blessing to include me. I could never be perfectly pure! There I stood, alone in that empty place with my human failures visible before him. For my heart is the place where my sins rest most heavily upon me. I felt estranged from God and from those I saw as being better than I. Standing in that empty place where I had defined perfection and purity as "not me," I knew I would never be able to see God!

I bowed my head—"Blessed are the pure in heart." O, how I long to be pure in heart! To hold only the good thoughts and protect them from perversion. To listen and not gossip. To be loving and obedient. To not be ruled by fear. To be nonjudgmental. To not limit myself and others. To not lie or manipulate. To be open and kind, tolerant and forgiving. To be good—not just some of the time but all the time. To be consistent and faithful. To live in community and not in isolation. To do unto others as I want them to do unto me! My constant prayer has been, "Create in me a pure heart, O God" (Psalm 51:10 NIV). A clean heart without any defects and deficits. O God, make me pure, make me better, make me worthy, make me whole, make me 100 percent.

Psalm 51 is the prayer David wrote after being chastised by Nathan for his rape of Bathsheba. (Read 2 Samuel 11–12 for the whole story.) David could not see beyond what he had wanted, and so he ignored what was right and what God would have him do. He lied, cheated, stole, and murdered in order to have Bathsheba, the wife of another man. Although we may not have done all that David did, our lives contain enough mistakes and missteps that are embarrassing in their own details. Embarrassing and human. Embarrassing and petty. Embarrassing and persistent. Embarrassing and life changing. Embarrassing and ultimately forgivable by God. Maybe I can be counted in this blessing of Jesus!

Maybe Jesus' blessing should not make me feel shame because of my human imperfections but remind me that I do not have the definitive statement on what is pure. God defines purity. And, God's grace is sufficient to make me pure. An encounter with Jesus sanctifies, purifies, perfects, and transforms us. It makes us whole and makes us enough. An encounter with Jesus changes us, makes our hearts pure in our humanness, and enables us to see God's image in ourselves and in others. My encounter with Jesus made me want to share the Good News with those who have not heard or who have forgotten. "O Lord, open my lips and my mouth will declare your praise. Then I will teach transgressors your ways and sinners will turn back to you" (Psalm 51:13, 15 NIV, paraphrase). I will teach them that, because of Jesus, even I am 100 percent pure! This is Good News!

Thought for the Day: Blessed are those who are pure in heart and those whom Jesus makes so!

Deborah Tinsley Taylor is a registered nurse, poet, singer, and liturgist. She has completed two years of seminary, taken a break, and will be returning to seminary as an exploring candidate for the ordained ministry in the United Methodist Church. Several of her poems are published in *Taking Back My Yesterdays* (1997), written by Linda H. Hollies.

Wilma H. Taylor

Break Me to Make Me . . . Break Me to Mold Me!

> *But you, beloved, build yourselves up on your most holy faith; pray in the Holy Spirit; keep yourselves in the love of God; look for the mercy of our Lord Jesus Christ unto eternal life. —Jude vv. 20–21 (RSV)*

As time progresses from the breaking of the water bag to the breaking of the vial of silver nitrate to aide in your ability to see, there are many forms of brokenness. When life begins its unexpected successions of encountered brokenness, you are a prime candidate to experience how to become all you believe you can be.

Sometimes the family structure is broken, leaving a void or a sense of something missing. And, we spend many aimless, searching years trying to fill the emptiness.

Sometimes, no matter how much effort is put forth to make you think differently, because of the lack of unity in the home, you continue to feel broken because of the splintered pieces of life.

I have found myself holding on to the splinters or broken pieces with the hope that one day a whole person would emerge from them. God knows that I want to be useful, not only to my own life; I also want to make a difference and have significant meaning in the lives of my family members, the society that I touch, and others, especially those who share in the Realm of God.

Even after accepting salvation, experiencing the in-dwelling or "filling" of the Holy Spirit, and receiving that special anointing used to destroy yokes in the lives of others, I kept searching. Through the years of study that goes with becoming a professional in my field and with the gift of wisdom that helps guide others through the maze of their life, my search continued. The feeling of being broken remained even when others dared to give me praise.

I finally arrived at the revelation that *God* was the one who was breaking me—in order to mold me into my most full potential! God had permitted all the years of searching to break my will and make me willing to become what God originally purposed for my life. Always God's hand was at work. Always God's plan was in effect. God had been there all the time! Thank *God* for knowing the road that I take and for letting me know and experience the reality that all things do work together for good of them that love the Lord and are called according to a divine purpose (Romans 8:28).

The searching was not in vain. I learned much along the way. And so I readily pray today, "Make me. Mold me after your perfect will."

Thought for the Day: Broken? The Potter is putting broken pieces back together again! Stop by and experience the remaking!

Wilma H. Taylor is founder and executive director of Wilma Taylor Ministries of Chicago, Illinois. With a special focus on youth and women, Wilma travels the world spreading the Good News of Jesus Christ. An international evangelist and a mother, Wilma is a member of The Church of God in Christ.

Daisybelle Thomas-Quinney

Staying Married: Ties That Bind

And remember, I am with you always, to the end of the age. —Matthew 28:20 (NRSV)

Why was I feeling so tired, lonely, and alone? I pondered as tears raced down my face. My husband sat across from me at the breakfast table in silence. My best friend was so close, yet I felt a deep emptiness. Was he with me or sitting by me? At that point, I began to sob loudly. Nelson gently inquired about the source of my tears and pain. How could I tell him that I felt he had abandoned me? I needed his company more. We were busy growing apart.

You must understand: Nelson is a jewel of a husband, who prides himself on taking care of as well as driving "Miss Daisy." December fifteenth will mark nine wonderful years of marriage. Our long-distance courtship between Michigan and Pennsylvania was a sheer twentieth century fairy-tale. He wooed me with cards every week and flowers as well as daily phone calls with prayer and funny songs. He loved to surprise me with unusual gifts, trips, and mystery games. He even drove to Alabama to ask my parents for my hand in marriage when I was forty-five years of beauty!

Our December wedding was a holiday pageant with eleven bridesmaids and groomsmen. My father, our local pastor, and my best Rev. Girl-friend, officiated at our wedding with guests from across the U.S.A. Students from my school sang. It was a day that Cinderella would have envied!

Nelson was an answer to prayer for help with my financial crisis. "God, please send me help," I prayed, realizing that my expenses exceeded my income. Several minutes later that same night, the phone rang. Nelson was calling from Pennsylvania to invite me to dinner the following weekend. I was livid! "God, how could you?" I argued. "I just prayed and you interrupted me with somebody I have no interest in whatsoever." The rest of the story is part of our nine years of love and the ties that bind us together.

My beloved has pampered, protected, and provided for me in wonderful ways. His love remains constant as he cooks, sometimes cleans, and attempts the laundry. Why the tears when I had what so many women dream about? Was my crying an act of selfishness? What more could he do or should I expect from him? Questions flooded my mind as the tears bathed my face.

We had been spending considerable time apart. He was doing his thing. I was going to work, retreats, performances, and women's conferences. What had happened to our quality time and fellowship? I realized that I missed my husband. I needed us to share all the little things that had brought us joy in the past. I wanted to laugh with him again! We were "together" whenever our paths crossed at the house, but the communion of our spirits was absent!

Genesis 2:24 states, "Therefore a man leaves his father and mother and clings to his wife, and they become one flesh." I needed oneness in our goals and aspirations, as well as sensuality! We were growing apart with our busy schedules.

Staying married requires constant attention to one another's needs. Nelson did not know how much I missed and needed quality time with him. Our spouses are not mind readers. We must learn how to communicate our true feelings to one another without accusing, blaming, or shaming. As a child, I observed my parents blaming and shaming instead of sharing what they really felt. Maybe they didn't know any better, but I decided my marriage would and could be different. Philippians 4:6 reminds us to "let your requests be made known."

From those tears at the breakfast table came conversation and comfort, resulting in a covenant to set aside each week a "just-for-us" day. Our first "just-for-us" day was truly fantastic! Real love answered my questions when we talked.

Thought for the Day: "Blessed be the ties that bind our hearts in Christian love. A fellowship of kindred minds is like to that above."

Daisybelle Thomas-Quinney, an ordained minister at Cedar Avenue Church of God, Sharon, Pennsylvania, is founder of Women in Ministry in the Shanango Valley. She is employed at Thiel College, Greenville, Pennsylvania, as coordinator of multicultural affairs and adjunct professor of religion with an M.Div. from Pittsburgh Theological Seminary. Having earned an M.A. in education from Louis National College of Education, Evanston, Illinois, and a B.A. in education from Stillman College, Tuscaloosa, Alabama, Daisybelle and her husband, Nelson Israel Quinney, II, are executive producers of her creative ministry, Voices of Freedom.

Sherry L. Townsend

Beyond My Will

And just then there appeared a woman with a spirit that had crippled her for eighteen years. She was bent over and was quite unable to stand up straight. When Jesus saw her, he called her over and said, "Woman, you are set free from your ailment." When he laid his hands upon her, immediately she stood up straight and began praising God. —Luke 13:11–13 (NRSV)

Think about how we wax floors in our homes. Normally, if there is significant buildup on the floor, we must strip away the buildup of old wax before putting down the new. If we want the floor to have that "see yourself " shine that we desire—no imperfections, smooth—taking up the old yellowing dull finish is a necessity.

This process of taking up the old finish is time-consuming and back-breaking work. It is not easy. This could explain why we are willing to either pay good money for products that claim that you can get the bright shining finish you want in just one step, or pay someone else to do it. However, the reality is that another person is not going to treat your stuff as you would. More than likely, after they finish you will find some smudges and streaks. Similarly, any of those products that claim to be able to make your work easier tend to leave a dull finish in the long run. Simply put, no matter how you look at it, you can not get around the hard work necessary to get the bright finish you desire.

Many of our lives, like some of our floors, have a build-up of life and its circumstances clouding our perspective. Fortunately for us, Jesus is able to deal with the stuff that clouds our perspectives and to lay new paths that shine through and through.

The passage in Luke 13:10–16 concerns a woman who has been bent over for eighteen years. We don't know how old she is, whether she is married or single, or if she has come to the synagogue alone. We know very little about her other than her condition—only that Satan has been giving her fits for eighteen years! We do know that she enters the synagogue and that, on this day like all the others before it, she is doubled over from the years of pain. She enters the synagogue requesting nothing and expecting nothing more than to hear the teachings.

The passage describes this woman as being *infirm*. A cursory glance at the passage might lead us to believe that she suffered a physical condition solely. But when the Greek word for *infirm* is studied in greater detail, we find that this reference is much deeper than we originally suspected. She is bent over physically, true enough, but her precarious position has probably been caused by the evil spirits to which she has been subjected. Those spirits may have been hurtful words, the spiteful behavior, or the negative thoughts of others.

Many of us are similarly afflicted. Societal pressures and oppression have crippled our minds and hearts. Often these pressures are so insidious that we fail to understand healing and feel that it is beyond us. Consider, however, that the infirm woman in Luke 13 still goes through the motions of coming to worship. How many times do I find myself just moving through the motions of life, even with my spiritual growth and development? Too often I have gone to church on Sunday because that is the acceptable time to go; to Bible study on Wednesday because it would look bad if I were not in attendance. Many of us go through our whole lives and spiritual development in this same way—as if we hear through "filtered" ears. Even when we arc offered liberation and healing, we still hear oppression and sickness.

For our sister in the synagogue, Jesus sees her need even while he is teaching. And Jesus speaks a word to her as well. Without preamble he says, "Woman, you are free." She has said not a word. She simply moves into the Savior's presence and is blessed. We can only speculate about her life prior to that day, but at that moment we are certain that she was in the presence of Jesus the Christ.

This passage points out that Jesus is constantly aware of us, our needs, concerns, cares, and complexities. In most cases the stuff that bends us over is beyond our capabilities to handle. But, Jesus is more than able to meet all of our needs.

This sister in the synagogue causes me to ponder: What paralyzes you and hinders your healing? When Jesus speaks a healing word to you, what do you hear? What "spirits" bend you over and burden you in this life? When has Jesus cut through your layers of doubt and unbelief to heal you beyond your will and your faith?

Thought for the Day: Dear Lord, help me to understand the power of Jesus Christ in my life and its ability to move beyond my comprehension. Help me to know that there are risks involved when healing takes place and that there are no layers that cannot be penetrated by the power of the risen Christ.

Sherry L. Townsend is an ordained elder in the United Methodist Church and presently serves as the director of education and teaching ministries as an associate council director in the Texas Annual Conference.

Brenda Bell Tribett

Reaching for the Prize

Not that I have already obtained this or have already reached the goal; but I press on to make it my own, because Christ Jesus has made me his own. Beloved, I do not consider that I have made it my own, but this one thing I do: forgetting what lies behind and straining forward to what lies ahead, I press on toward the goal for the prize of the heavenly call of God in Christ Jesus. —Philippians 3:12–14 (NRSV)

When I was a little girl, I liked to buy Cracker Jacks. You could purchase a box for only a nickel. Not only did you get the caramel flavored popcorn and peanuts, but you also got a prize. The prize was usually near the bottom of the box. Because I was eager to reach the prize, I would open the box from the bottom. My goal was to reach the prize! I didn't want to wait until I had eaten all of the popcorn; I wanted to discover the exciting, new toy inside.

So it is in life. Many of us strive to reach the prize. We set our goals early in life. Many young sisters strive to reach the prize, but they want it *now*! They don't want to work through the struggles to reach their goal. They have grown up in a microwave generation where everything is instantaneous. They have set their goals, but oftentimes they don't want to work their way to the top. They want to start out at the top. They want to wear the top of the line in designer clothes. They want to drive the top of the line in cars. They want the prize now. I know. Been there. And, done that!

When I fail to reach the goal that I have set for myself, I become frustrated. I have seen many of the challenges in my life as obstacles, rather than opportunities to grow and mature. I have been frustrated with relationships, with my status in life, with my achievements, and with the personal or material possessions that I have attained. When I feel that I have not reached my goal, I feel like a failure, that I have missed success! In reality, many times I have failed to recognize that this "failure" has been my blessing! God often prepares me for a greater blessing through the hard work and the struggles that are necessary to reach my goal. The prize comes when I reach the bottom!

I have discovered that trials and struggles help to make us strong. The challenges make us more appreciative. We develop character and patience because of our experiences. The prize is worth the wait. Our ultimate goal as Christians is the prize in Jesus Christ. Whatever our goals in life may be, we must remember that we cannot reach them on our own. We must press forward in Jesus Christ, knowing, loving, and serving, believing in him, focusing on him, and striving to reach our goal.

Thought for the Day: Dear God, as I strive to reach the prize, help me to see today's challenges as opportunities to grow and mature in your Word. Grant me humility, commitment, and tenacity to wait on you.

Brenda Bell Tribett serves as director of Black Church Education and director of Children's Ministries for American Baptist Churches, USA. She is a native of Richmond, Virginia, and has one daughter and one granddaughter.

Roberta L. Walker

No "I Do"
If God Doesn't

So they are no longer two, but one flesh. Therefore what God has joined together, let no one separate. —Matthew 19:6 (NRSV)

As God uses me to minister to African American women at church, home, and school, I'm amazed at the number of sisters who struggle daily with unhappy marriages. I know that work is required to maintain any relationship. I even think it reasonable to expect that, at times, the work required will become difficult. I cannot, however, believe that God intends for struggle in a marriage to become the norm rather than the exception.

Having struggled every year for eleven years in my own marriage, I often wondered whether to continue the fight. Reared in a traditional Baptist church, I had always been taught to do whatever was necessary to hold the marriage together. But I had to ask myself, and even ask God, "When is enough ever enough?" Does God, who is the source of my joy, require me to remain in an unhappy marriage?

In Matthew 19:6, God reveals the strength of a holy union. Here we see the true glue that binds and holds a relationship together: God becomes the cement that makes the bond of marriage inseparable. The Word lets us know that when God joins man and woman, they become one flesh. Only when God joins the couple is there that blessed assurance that the marriage will remain intact.

Too often we put ourselves into relationships rather than waiting for God to join us. Many times, we marry because we are pressured by family members, because we feel that we are at the age where we should be married, or because we are lonely but don't wish to sleep around. The latter was my experience; I reached out to a friend for companionship while nursing a broken heart. Confusing loneliness for love, I applied the Scripture, "It is better to marry than to be aflame with passion" (1 Corinthians 7:9

NRSV). Wanting to do the right thing, I consented to marriage. I heeded the recorded word of God but did not seek a direct word as to whether or not this was the man for me to marry. When we fail to consult God, we too often do the wrong thing for the "right" reason!

Shortly after I was called into ministry, I became a full-time student in a weekend seminary program. My husband wasn't able to support me in this journey. He filed for divorce. The Scripture that God gave to me then, I wish to give to my sisters still living within the struggle. First Corinthians 7:10–16 is the total context, but the specific verse that God helped me to hold on to was verse 15, which states, "But if the unbelieving partner separates, let it be so; in such a case the brother or sister is not bound. It is to peace that God has called you." Above all else, God wants us to be at peace.

At the same time, this Scripture is not an excuse to go from relationship to relationship. None of us should make any decision about marriage without first consulting God. Whether married or single, sisters, you should seriously consider the far-reaching effects of being mismatched with unbelievers (2 Corinthians 6:14). Please know that a man's church attendance does not assure his being saved. Always ask God first before committing to a relationship! If God does not give consent, neither should you. When asked how to avoid an unhappy marriage, I say, "An ounce of prevention is worth a pound of cure."

Thought for the Day: I will neither enter nor exit any relationship without God's consent.

Roberta L. Walker is associate minister at Westwood Baptist Church in Richmond, Virginia, where she serves as minister of Christian education. She is a second-year student at the Samuel Dewitt Proctor School of Theology at Virginia Union University. Roberta has an M.Ed. and serves as a teacher trainer for Richmond City Public Schools.

Joyce E. Wallace

Paroled or Pardoned?

> *Now God declares us "not guilty" of offense if we trust in Jesus Christ, who in his kindness freely takes away our sins. —Romans 3:24 (TLB)*

Have you ever found yourself living as if you were on parole? Living as a parolee means being subjected to restrictive conditions, human-constructed impositions, and powerlessness. To be on parole is to live every day with guilt and unforgiveness.

The opposite of parole is pardon. Being fully pardoned is living in freedom with all the rights, privileges, and power that go with freedom. Being pardoned is to live every day within the grace of God.

However, when we fall short of the expectations of others and are made to feel worthless;

when we get so caught up in the negatives and can't see the good in ourselves; when in the light of the tangible results of past mistakes, we can't forgive ourselves—then we lose sight of the distinction between a parole and a pardon and waffle between them. I know because I have been there!

From time to time along my spiritual journey, I have forgotten one of the most important messages the Bible has for us, that we are justified by God's grace through our faith in Christ Jesus, whose payment for our sins has wiped away our guilt. These lapses of memory have caused me many hours of disenchantment with myself. During some of these periods I played hostess to highly successful "pity" parties where Satan was the guest of honor! I endured costly visits to therapists and medical doctors due to the emotional stress and physical pains I created by beating up on myself with the guilty *shouldas, couldas,* and *oughtas.* And then there were the countless "potential" accomplishments that I allowed ole picture-perfect procrastination to keep me from starting, following through on, or finishing.

And, while I was wasting that precious time and missing those pregnant opportunities by chastising myself; while I was seeking permission *to do* from places and people other than God;

while I was absorbing others' criticisms and complaints as if they knew best who and what I could be in Christ Jesus, I was living like a parolee instead of as the fully pardoned twinkling star that I am through God's grace! Only when I accept God's grace can I practice self-forgiveness, affirm my own gifts, experience inner peace, practice the power and possibility, and be motivated to take actions that make a difference.

So, when you are tempted to live like a parolee through self-condemnation, internalizing unwarranted accusations and experiencing memory lapses—remember me! Then, remember to seek the word of God in Romans 3 and reclaim your full pardon. The ransom has been paid in full with the blood of Jesus!

Thought for the Day: Forgive yourself and live each day fully in God's grace, peace, and power.

Joyce E. Wallace is a graduate of the University of Missouri at Columbia with a B.S. in merchandising and business management, and she holds an M.Div. from St. Paul School of Theology. She is the pastor of Conant Avenue United Methodist Church in Detroit and serves as secretary for the Black Clergywomen of the United Methodist Church. Joyce's ministry focus is on pastoral care and counseling to assist others in becoming "Twinkling Stars"!

Elaine P. Walters

The Person Called Woman

> *I will praise thee; for I am fearfully and wonderfully made: marvelous are thy works; and that my soul knoweth right well.* —*Psalm 139:14 (KJV)*

My journey to womanhood was rough and rugged. My journey to womanhood was filled with chuck holes. My journey to womanhood was really bumpy. I got lost trying to find the person called "woman." I looked for her in the females of my family, my neighborhood, my church, in magazines, and on billboards. When I was growing up, a "real" woman was voluptuous. She had curvy hips, big legs, and an ample bosom. At age twelve I stood five feet nine inches tall, weighed ninety pounds, and had a flat chest. At age twenty-one things had only improved slightly. I weighed 114 pounds and wore bra size 32A. I looked at all the other women around me and concluded that I was a mutation or at least a cruel joke.

Little Richard released "Long Tall Sally" and "Bony Maroni" just so my friends could torment me! My uncle reminded me every chance he got, "No one wants a bone but a dog." Like most people with low self-esteem, I tried to compensate with behaviors that were sure to be noticed. You bet I attracted some dogs.

But one day, I don't recall exactly when, my breakthrough came. I heard the words of the psalmist, "I am fearfully and wonderfully made." Oh, I didn't praise God immediately, nor did I know it right well, but my appetite was stimulated. I began a search that enabled me to discover that God had delighted in making me and had been extraordinarily careful in every detail. I came to know my Creator as a loving God who had made me beautiful in every way. I lifted up my bowed head and began to give God the glory!

We live in a society filled with merchants arrogant enough to presume to define standards of beauty. But mothers and sisters and daughters of the Most High God, make no doubt about it; you are a masterpiece. You are an original. You were custom made. You have got to understand that God delights in you as divine handiwork. Did I learn the lesson well? Did I write it upon the tablet of my heart? Girlfriend, you ought to see me now! Throw your head back and declare, "Marvelous is this work!"

Thought for the Day: The journey to becoming is rough. But the Divine Designer constructed you with lasting beauty!

Elaine P. Walters is the assistant pastor and administrator at St. Paul A.M.E. Church, Indianapolis, Indiana, where her spouse, Walter, is pastor. She is the executive director of Indiana One Church, One Child Program, Inc., and an adjunct faculty member at Martin University. She is an ordained itinerant elder in the African Methodist Episcopal Church, a Certified Clinical Social Worker in the state of Indiana, and a mother.

Leah E. White

Keep Focused

Finally, sisters, whatsoever things are true, whatsoever things are honest, whatsoever things are just, whatsoever things are pure, whatsoever things are lovely, whatsoever things are of good report; if there be any virtue, and if there be any praise, think on these things. —Philippians 4:8 (KJV)

Today, I was sitting at my desk trying to get a few things done. However, I could not focus. There were too many things running through my mind. I felt like a train speeding into Grand Central Station. My mind was racing at speeds of over one hundred miles per minute and I was going too fast to pull into the station to pick up any passengers! As soon as one thought would enter the corner of my mind, another would race around the bend so quickly that I'd pass the previous thought by.

I was moving so fast that the blessings of God were vanishing before my very eyes, unnoticed. I had become too absorbed in my failures, my mistakes, my troubles, my trials, and my conflicts of yesterday to appreciate all of my victories and my miracles of the present. Regretfully, the marvelous blessings that God sent my way went unnoticed because my mind was too crowded to appreciate God's presence in my midst. Much like the seed that was planted in the thorny ground, the blessings of God were being choked out of my memory banks.

I had to learn how to heed the advice of the apostle Paul, who encourages us to saturate our minds with good things. Focus on the positives and not the negatives. Easily said, but difficult to achieve. But everything worth achieving has never been easy. Most valuable things come with struggle.

If I desire peace and joy in my life, I must struggle to keep the clutter of negativity out. That will require my being selective in who I allow in my sphere today! I will have to be on alert about who enters my emotional zones. When threatening and depressing thoughts try to bombard me, I must immediately erect, "no trespassing" signs around the borders of my mind. I cannot allow myself to become distracted by the trite and the insignificant! I am learning to let go of the "things" of yesterday.

Much of yesterday I cannot change. Those things belong in the history files. Some need to be moved to the archives of my memory banks. Others need to be trashed and "deleted." Nothing can be allowed to consume more memory than it deserves! I must learn to change what I can, accept what I can't, and learn the difference between the two. I am wasting valuable time and energy rehearsing conversations with persons who have gone on to other matters. I am rendering myself useless when I preoccupy myself with matters that are out of my control. I am subjecting myself to tyranny when I surround myself with persons who do not have a positive outlook on life.

I desire to live the healthy, happy, and fulfilled life that God has planned for me. So I must guard my space. I must protect my time. I must be selective with my company. For I become subject to those things which surround me or become a part of my environment. I must not allow them to consume my mind. I must guard each corridor with good, and pleasant, and virtuous, and lovely thoughts. For God has promised: "God will keep her in perfect peace, whose mind is stayed on thee: because she trusts in me" (Isaiah 26:3).

Thought for the Day: Guard your mind!

Leah E. White is a native Baltimorean born to James L. Mosley and Dr. Mary A. Phillips. Currently, she is bi-vocational, serving as Pastor of the Greater Faith Baptist Church and administrator of the New Psalmist Christian School. She is supported by a loving husband, Russell E. White, one son, Jeffrey and his wife, Donna, and their son Jeffrey Jr.

Marsha Brown Woodard

And the Sisters Danced

Then the prophet Miriam, Aaron's sister, took a tambourine in her hand; and all the women went out after her with tambourines and with dancing.
—Exodus 15:20 (NRSV)

After they had crossed the Red Sea, the sisters joined Miriam in a dance and a time of praise. It was a dance of thanksgiving. It was a dance of joy. It was a dance in spite of all they had gone through. When God had moved on their behalf, their response was not, "Why did it take so long?" Instead the sisters picked up tambourines, grabbed friends, and danced!

Today we need to dance. In spite of all that we are going through, as women we need a dance. We need a dance of thanksgiving. We should have a dance of praise.

To dance we need memory. We need to know and remember our experiences. We also need to be able to see God in the midst of our daily living. When we can see God, then we remember that it is not of our own strength that we accomplish anything. It is God interceding for us. And when God does a great work, confounds our enemies, and makes liars of those who have said to us it could not, would not, and should not be done—we ought to dance!

When the "horse and the rider" of our experience has drowned in the Red Sea, we need to break out in a dance. The horse and the rider for you may be the person who lied to you, or the one who betrayed you, or the one who tried to get you fired, or even the one who fired you! It may be the past that has seemed to haunt you, or the habit you haven't been able to break. It is whatever has been in control of your life! When God drowns "it" for you, you ought to dance.

For, when the "horse and the rider" is gone, you are free. Now, the future is different; it will be written in a new way. Sister, pick up that tambourine. Sister, put on those dancing shoes, and

Girl, get ready. For God *is* moving on your behalf! God *is* doing a great work. God is removing every hindering force. And, when you look up, all that you thought could not be *will* be! God *is* doing the seemingly impossible just for you. So dance, Sister. Dance! Dance! Dance!

Thought for the Day: God is moving on your behalf doing great and wonderful things. Dance!

Marsha Brown Woodard serves as an adjunct professor at Eastern Baptist Theological Seminary. She is the president of the Ministers Council of the Philadelphia Baptist Association and resides in Wayne, Pennsylvania.

Betty Wright-Riggins

Spinach Spirituality

But you will receive power when the Holy Spirit has come upon you. . . .
—*Acts 1:8*

Do you remember the cartoon character Popeye? Recently it has occurred to me the spiritual truths inherent in that cartoon series. "I'm Popeye the sailor man," he would say. "I'm Popeye the sailor man. I yam what I yam. I'm Popeye the sailor man."

Popeye always seemed to know where his strength lay. He was absolutely clear that the power to overcome obstacles, the power to stand in the mist of confusion and adversity, resided in a power much bigger than him. It rested in a can of spinach.

I remember as a child my grandmother would make me eat spinach. Grandma said spinach was good for me. It had vitamins to grow my hair, build my bones, make my skin smooth, and put a twinkle in my eyes. "Don't you want to be like Popeye?" she would say. When I was a child, spinach had power.

Spinach empowered Popeye. The Scripture affirms for us that our strength to overcome is in the power of the Holy Spirit. Jesus said the Holy Spirit would advocate for us. The Holy Spirit will guide us into all truth and will mirror Christ's glory.

Have you noticed that even though there was power in the can of spinach for Popeye, the power never worked until he reached for it, held it, and ingested it? Spinach was power for Popeye only when he allowed it to move on the inside of him. A word of insight for us is to allow the Holy Spirit to take up residence in us and to control us.

Many of us say we believe in the power of the Holy Spirit. Yet we are uncomfortable with allowing anything to control us. Some of us are fearful God might challenge our comfortable places, shake up our programs, or interrupt our well-ordered lives. So we choose to keep the Holy Spirit at arm's length, just outside of our inner selves. Let us not live Popeye's words, "I yam what I yam." But let us affirm that we can be and do all things through Christ who strengthens us.

Thought for the Day: Come abide in me, Holy Spirit. Fill me with your strength and power.

Betty Wright-Riggins is former Director of school at Cornerstone Christian Academy, Philadelphia, Pennsylvania. At present, she is adjunct professor at Eastern Baptist Theological Seminary, also in Philadelphia, Pennsylvania.

Riene Adams-Morris

Afterword

Now may the God of peace, that brought again from the dead our Lord Jesus, that great shepherd of the sheep, through the blood of the everlasting covenant, make us all perfect in every good work to do the will of God (Hebrews 13:20–21 KJV). It is the divine will that you go forth in prayer and in power seeking your sisters, to bless them and to be blessed by them through Jesus Christ, to whom be glory and honor forever and ever.

Always remember that it is because of the Divine will and grace that — *the Sisters gather!*

Linda H. Hollies

The Last Word

The Sisters have gathered! Each one of us has stirred in a dose of healing balm for your journey, for we have opened ourselves to allow you to know our struggles, our pains, our prayers, and the processes that have brought us "thus far along the way."

God is yet working in us, on us, with us, and now through us to dispense a dollop of salve for discouraged souls. The collective wisdom of this particular group of wounded healers is powerful enough to have long-lasting effects *if* you follow directions well.

Usually medicines that attack deadly viruses and bacteria come in a liquid form that needs to be refrigerated and safely stored. Since this medication is for the healing of souls, it is necessary for you to consume it slowly. Read it and reread it. Then meditate upon what you've read so that its insights might be stored and sealed within your very spirit.

Take it daily. As you practice the spiritual disciplines of Scripture reading, reflection, and prayer, take a few extra minutes to swallow the advice of a Sister who has "been there and done that" very thing you're facing today. If you can, practice what she teaches as it applies to your life.

Normal prescriptions say, "Shake well before using." However, with this spiritual healing balm, you take first and shake later! The shaking comes with the joyful realization that another Sister shares your story, knows your pain, and has lived to tell it after the storm. The shaking comes with your deliverance from old yokes that have kept you "sick" for too long. The shaking comes with the uncontrollable and unrestrainable praise that will burst forth from your lips as you give God the glory for this "Balm in Gilead"!

The book has ended. Yet we will never part. For the Sisterhood has opened their lives to you. You have allowed us access to your very "is-ness." Now we are one. The story continues. The healing will be passed on. But now it's your turn to gather the Sisterhood!

Shalom, beloved Sisters!

Sista Linda

Index of Topics

Family

Grief

Inspirational

Knowing God

Loving Ourselves/Self-Knowledge

Marriage

Overcoming Hardship

Sisterhood